Every Body Is a Sexy Body

*Improving Sexual Satisfaction
Through Body Image*

Annette Lee, PhD

Copyright © 2024: All rights reserved.

No part of this publication may be copied, reproduced in any format, by any means, electronic or otherwise, without prior consent from the copyright owner and publisher of this book.

Contents

Introduction 4

CHAPTER 01.
Being Present: Get Out of Your Head and Into Your Bed 11

CHAPTER 02.
Connecting – Becoming One with Ourselves and Others 25

CHAPTER 03.
Intimacy – Getting Close to Yourself to Get Closer to Others 39

CHAPTER 04.
Communication - Let's Talk About Sex...and Bodies 52

CHAPTER 05.
Authenticity - Be Yourself, Be Yourself! 65

CHAPTER 06.
Transcendence and Personal Transformation – Rising Above ..80

CHAPTER 07.
If You Can't Have Fun, What's the Sense in Doing It? 95

CHAPTER 08.
Vulnerability – Letting Yourself Be Seen 108

Conclusion 121

Endnotes 124

Appendix A: Grounding Skills 128

Appendix B: Mental Health Resources 130

Appendix C: Book Recommendations by Chapter 131

Appendix D: Additional Resources by Chapter 134

Introduction

I love Italy. I love the vibe, the food, the people, and the language (even though I only know approximately ten words, none of which make any sense spoken together – it just sounds beautiful). The beauty, the history, the scenery. The beaches, the mountains, the islands, the cities, and the countryside. The simultaneous rushing about and slowing down. One of my dreams is to be able to live there someday – even if it is just temporary.

You are probably wondering why I am starting off a book about body image and sexual satisfaction by writing about my love for Italy. Good question. The answer is bikinis. In Italy, all women wear bikinis. Tall, thin women. Short, fat women. Young, toned women. Old, flabby women. ALL WOMEN. I struggle with body image to this day. Maybe it's not okay to admit on page one of a book designed to improve body image that it's not something that I think will ever fully go away– but seeing all the bikinis on all of the different bodies in Italy was life-changing for me. I was amazed, impressed, and, most of all, inspired. If these women could feel so comfortable in their own skin – these women who live in the world of Versace, Prada, Gucci, and Armani – then why couldn't I?

Seeing all those different bodies in bikinis on Italian beaches didn't solve my body image issues. But it did do one important thing. It pushed me to start challenging my thoughts around body image standards. And then, I started to look at my behaviors and change them in small ways. These were not radical changes by any means. For some women, they are everyday, regular things. They were things like starting to wear make-up beyond a simple mascara. Things like buying clothing I liked without worrying how it might look on my body shape, but rather focusing on how I felt in it. I even bought a bikini! Did the thoughts still come into my mind about how my hips were too wide, how I had too much cellulite, or how big my butt was? Of course. But, I used the exercises that I have taught clients over the years (which I will share with you in this book) to manage those thoughts in a healthier way, and I did the things anyway. Did it help that I did these things during a global pandemic when I didn't have to go out in public very often? Of course. But I was able to use that time to "practice" feeling comfortable in my body, and when we emerged from lockdown, I wore that bikini to the beach.

So, where does sex come into the picture? When you aren't feeling comfortable in your body, or you're going to the beach and wearing tons of layers that cause you to sweat and be uncomfortable, you don't really feel sexy. At least, I don't. But by shedding some of those clothing layers and letting myself feel freer, I started to feel sexier. I started to pay more attention to my body, including what it wanted and what gave it pleasure. I became more willing to share these things with my partner and to ask for new and different things in the bedroom. This is how I hope that this book will be helpful for you. By improving your body image, I hope that you can also have a more satisfying sex life.

Before we get to that, let me tell you why I'm writing this book. I am a licensed mental health counselor (LMHC) and sex therapist who has been practicing in the State of New York for over ten years. Since becoming an LMHC, I have worked in a variety of settings. Most of my experience was spent in community mental health clinics and in my own private practice. One thing that has been consistent throughout my work is that I have repeatedly met clients who, at some point during our time together, end up sharing with me their negative body image issues. It did not matter their age. It did not matter their sexual orientation, their race, or their sex assigned at birth. It did not even matter their size, their weight, or their body type. Nearly every single woman I have ever worked with – or even known personally for that matter – has expressed to me disliking at least one part of their body – and even sometimes their whole bodies. When I dug deeper with these clients, they would share with me how that negative body image impacted their sex life. And it was not impacting it in a good way, either. I could really relate to those clients.

For as long as I can remember, I've struggled with how I feel about my body. Back as far as childhood, when I was certainly not obese or even overweight, I was keenly aware of not wanting to look different, be too large, or take up too much space. It certainly didn't get better when I did gain weight. Even now, writing this book to help others, I still struggle. When I would hear women tell me about how they would shield certain body parts from their partner(s) or only make love under the blankets or with the lights off, I would truly understand that shame-driven behavior. Like my clients, I have also experienced thoughts of hating my body and have viewed myself as gross or disgusting because I have cellulite and flab. I have tried to hide my body from my partner, and I have denied myself sexual pleasure for weeks at a time because I was certain that my body wasn't sexy enough. Hearing this echoed by my clients and learning that this was such a universal experience, I knew it was something I had to do more to help with. After a lot of research and thought about what would and would not help, I've compiled a collection of resources that I have shared in this book. These resources will help you do just that – experience better sex through an improved body image.

First, let me share a little more about me. I am 40-something, married, white, cis-gendered female, queer-identified femme, upper middle class, atheist, fat but able-bodied, and monogamous. I live in a rural area in a blue state, and I am the first and only member of my family so far to attend anything beyond trade school. I am also a dog mom and a lover of books, crystals, and nature. I have an insatiable wanderlust and love exploring different places – meeting their people, learning how they live, eating their foods, and seeing the beauty in new places. I especially love waterfalls, mountains, and beaches. I love football – specifically the Buffalo Bills, with whom I have had a seriously unhealthy relationship for over 30 years. I also have a weakness for reality TV and Vampire dramas. If you meet me at a conference or at a party, you will probably think I'm quiet and maybe a little stuck up, but if you crack my introverted shell and start a conversation with me, I probably won't stop talking and will ask you a million questions about yourself. I love to learn, and even more, I love to understand.

Many of you are probably wondering why in the world you would need to know all that. It's a fair question. I am sharing these things about me because I want to be transparent and honest about the lens through which I am writing. Through all the components that combine to form my identity, I have accumulated a specific experience and understanding of body image and sexual satisfaction that will be very different from yours. Our identities are so much more than just our gender, our age, our race, our social class, our education level, our sexual orientation, or our disability status. Each part of who we are intersects to create a unique and special individual, and no book will ever be able to truly speak to all our uniqueness. By honoring our differences and being transparent about who I am, I hope to give you the information and space that you need to be able to make an informed decision about taking this journey with me.

Like most of us, some parts of who I am are privileged, and some are oppressed. Talking about privilege may seem out of place in a book about body image and sexual pleasure, but a major component of our body images and the ways that we experience sex come from where we "fit" within certain societal hierarchies. In our society, whether we like it or not (and I don't), a hierarchy exists regarding every single aspect of identity. This hierarchy essentially dictates who is dominant over who or who is "better" than who, including who meets the beauty standards and who does not. The more oppressed identities we have, the more different and away from the standard we feel. Connecting our identities to sex recognizes that the hierarchy also dictates who is worthy of experiencing pleasure and who is not. For example, in my case, the hierarchy says that because I am white, cis-gendered, and able-bodied, I am worthy of certain things, including pleasure, but at the same time, it says because I am fat, queer, and a woman, I am not worthy. Talk about confusing!

Sadly, the confusion and the unhappiness that come with aspects of our identity end up keeping us stuck in a space where we dislike ourselves. This sometimes even results in us buying products designed to solve the problems associated with the parts of our identity which are less than. I know I, for one, have spent boatloads of money trying to "fix" my fatness.

Understanding our identities also helps us to understand what I will refer to in this book as "the messaging." The messaging is a simple way to identify all the various inputs that we experience from birth that collectively inform the way that we feel about our bodies and our sexual experiences. Think of it like cooking a pot of vegetable soup – the messaging is the ingredients portion of the recipe – the potatoes, the carrots, the beans, the corn, the tomatoes – each ingredient represents a piece of the messaging that you received at some point in your life that came together in the pot to determine what your soup would taste like – or how you individually would feel about your body and your sex life. If you grew up in a conservatively religious household that didn't believe in sex outside of marriage, if you were exposed to Hallmark movies with romantic messages about love and relationships, if you had a parent who was constantly dieting or nitpicking what you ate, if you read in Cosmo the best way to have mind-blowing sex, or if you were made to believe that the supermodel body was the only body that could be sexy or beautiful- these are all parts of the messaging. So are the pieces of our identities. If we are black or white, if we are gay or straight, if we are disabled, or if we grew up poor or in a small, rural town – all of this influences the messaging that we were exposed to. Remember those clients I told you about? The ones with poor body image that impacted their sex lives? That body image didn't just come out of nowhere. It came from the messaging.

Speaking of identities, I need to make a caveat here. There is an incredibly wide diversity of women that exists, and it would be impossible for me to pretend that this book will meet the needs of every single woman. What I will do is attempt to include as many diverse examples as possible and acknowledge any challenges that certain women or identities might have with specific exercises and concepts.

What is body image anyway? Body image is defined as a combination of a person's view of their physical self and the thoughts and feelings that result from that view. Like body image, our sexual self-schema also developed in part from the messaging. Sexual self-schemas are essentially how we think and feel about our sexual selves, our sex lives, and how we view things like pleasure. As I learned through my experience and my work with clients, body image has a big impact on our sexual self-schemas. Those pesky worries about our bodies all have the potential to reduce our sexual satisfaction. The specific worries are endless, and it would be impossible for me to create a definitive list in this book. They include things like cellulite, being too bony or skinny, being fat, the size of breasts and other body parts, having saggy body parts or skin, scars, genital appearance or smells, hip dips, facial features, wrinkles, stray hairs, and on and on and on.

There might be some difficult thoughts and feelings that emerge as you read this book. Exploring the messaging and the impact that it has had on the way we feel about our bodies and our sexualities isn't exactly a walk in the park. You might find yourself feeling angry, frustrated, helpless, or hopeless at times during this process. You very likely are going to be facing feelings of shame straight in the eye. You will have to be honest with yourself about how your thoughts and feelings impact your behaviors and dig deep to identify what you are willing and able to change. None of this is easy work. But it is worthy work. And I believe that doing the work as openly and honestly as you are able will be transformative. Because of the potential challenges involved with this work, I have included some emotional regulation and grounding skills in Appendix A. If you find yourself struggling beyond what basic coping skills can help with, please reach out to a therapist who can help guide you through the process. In Appendix B, I've included resources to help you do this if needed.

While I believe that this book can help women, I also strongly subscribe to a person-centered approach. This means that I believe each one of you reading this book already knows what you need. And you may or may not need every single tool that I am going to share with you. Please feel free to take what you need from this book and leave the rest. Skip sections that don't apply to you and your experience. Immerse yourself deeply in the ones that do. Use the resources in the appendices to explore more fully the topics and concepts that speak to you. Write in it, highlight it, tear it apart -do whatever you need to do with it to make this book work for you.

One last thing before we dive into the good stuff. Sexual satisfaction is a subjective experience. Everyone is going to have a different idea of what sexual satisfaction means to them. It's as unique to us as our identities are. To help make sense of sexual satisfaction and keep things as objective as possible, I am using a couple of different guideposts. The main way in which sexual satisfaction will be viewed is by considering what Peggy Kleinplatz and her colleagues identified through their research in 2009 as the factors of great sex: being present, connection with partner, sexual and erotic intimacy, communication, empathy, authenticity, transcendence, exploration, fun, and vulnerability. Peggy and one of her colleagues, A. Dana Ménard, wrote a book, *Magnificent Sex: Lessons from Extraordinary Lovers,* which dives much deeper into each component than I will and is highly recommended as an additional resource.

I will also be keeping a pleasure-over-performance view, which is something that has emerged as a key concept in sex therapy over the last decade or so. Pleasure over performance recognizes that most of the messaging has told us that pleasure comes exclusively from orgasms. The problem with this limited view is that it does not encompass the multitude of ways in which women experience sexual and sensual pleasure, which we will explore throughout the book. Further problematic, this view frames sexual encounters in a performance-based way – sex becomes a pass/fail activity. In other words, if you cannot have an orgasm, then you are failing at sex. When linked with body image, it can be perceived as yet another failure. Suddenly, we are failing at how we look AND how we perform sexually. I don't know about you, but for me, that hasn't felt great. Are you ready to challenge the messaging, find ways to improve your body image, and have a more pleasurable sex life? Let's get started!

CHAPTER ONE

Being Present: Get Out of Your Head and Into Your Bed

What is Mindfulness

Chances are that at some point over the last ten years, you have heard the term "mindfulness." It has been such a big buzzword that it seems like an entire industry has sprung up around it. It has been on the cover of magazines – in fact, there is an actual magazine named *Mindful* – and there are countless books, journals, apps, videos, and websites devoted to teaching this practice. There's a good reason for it being so widespread: mindfulness is so beneficial that I teach it to nearly every client I work with. However, despite its popularity, most people don't know much about mindfulness, and those who do struggle with implementing it in a consistent and meaningful way. When I introduce it to my clients, I let them know that mindfulness is an easy but difficult concept that takes A LOT of practice to master.

There are many definitions out there, but the most straightforward way I have found to describe it is this: mindfulness is being in the moment nonjudgmentally. That's it. That's what makes it easy. The challenge comes from our own brains. One of the major functions of the brain is to control thought. There is some debate around just how many thoughts we experience per day, but the most recent research puts that number at around 6,000 – which boils down to 6.5 thoughts per minute when you factor in 8 hours of sleep per day[1]. That's a lot!! The problem is that many of those thoughts have nothing to do with the moment we are currently in. They have to do with what we did this morning, last week, or even ten years ago. They have to do with what we are worried about, what might happen in the meeting we have in ten minutes, or where we might be in ten years. Being in the moment requires us to let go of those thoughts, not to judge them, and to focus purely on what is right now. That is the difficult part.

Another challenge with being mindful comes from the messaging. The messaging tells us that we are supposed to be anything but mindful. Have you ever described yourself as a multitasker? Yeah, me too. In fact, I used to be incredibly proud of this description and boasted about it on cover letters and in interviews. In a world where the demands on women are seemingly endless – everything from work to school to parenting to maintaining a household (whether that is just you or a family), to taking care of ourselves mentally and physically to socializing – we are encouraged to multitask to be effective and do everything we need to do. Talk on the phone to your friend while you cook dinner. Do the dishes and clean the kitchen while you help the kids with their homework. Even something that might not overtly feel like multitasking, such as mentally running through your day's schedule while taking a shower in the morning, is something that takes us away from being mindful. As you can see from these examples, multitasking is essentially the enemy of mindfulness. Multitasking takes away from our ability to be effective – how well can you really connect with your friend if you're focusing on not burning your dinner?

Let's talk briefly about the not judging part of mindfulness because I think this often gets lost in the shuffle of focusing on the here and now. I personally believe that judging our thoughts has become so common and automatic that we don't even notice when we are doing it. A common example of this is "shoulding," or thinking about what we should or shouldn't be doing, thinking, or feeling. Any time a "should" shows up in our thoughts, it is a judgment. But shoulding happens so often that we don't even realize that we are doing it. Not judging means letting go of the shoulds and the should-nots. It means accepting what you are thinking and feeling without beating yourself up for it. When we stop judging the moment, we are also embracing a willingness to participate in the moment regardless of what is happening and regardless of what we are thinking and feeling about it. This means that being mindful isn't always a pleasant experience. But without that discomfort, we cannot reap the benefits of mindfulness.

Why Practice Mindfulness?

As I mentioned, I teach mindfulness techniques to nearly every client I work with. I do this because I strongly believe that it is the building block to improving our overall mental health. Once we can be in the moment more frequently, we start to gain control over our thoughts and our emotions by actively deciding what is needed in the here and now. Our emotional intelligence increases because we can identify exactly what we are thinking, what we are feeling, and how those thoughts and feelings are contributing to our behaviors. This allows for intentionality and purpose in our actions and helps us to move away from feeling like our thoughts and emotions are controlling us. After all, how can we best decide what is needed at this exact moment if we are too focused on what happened this morning or if we are worried about what might happen this evening?

Another benefit of mindfulness is it helps us gain an awareness of our internal state. If we are not bogged down by all sorts of random thoughts, we can really start to pay attention to what is happening in our bodies in that moment. This interoceptive awareness, or bodily attunement, can let us know what feels good or what does not feel good. From a sexual perspective, this allows us to focus more on pleasure in our bodies instead of worrying about the result of a sexual encounter. Have you ever been so focused on wondering if the orgasm is coming that it never does? That's because you weren't being mindful.

Being present, focused, and embodied is the first element that Kleinplatz and her cohorts identified in their study as a major component of great sex[2]. This is described by study participants as being totally absorbed in the moment. Sound familiar? It is what we have just been discussing as the basic elements of mindfulness. One of the consequences of not being mindful is that we disengage from our experiences. If we disengage during sex, we aren't likely to enjoy our experience. Being unmindful can cause us to feel unsure about what we are doing sexually and to have difficulty identifying what we need or want out of our sexual experiences. And when all of this happens, we can experience an overall disinterest in sex altogether. Tuning back into our bodies and paying attention to what feels good can help us rekindle that interest. By exploring our bodies in a mindful way, even on a solo basis, we can remind ourselves of what pleasure feels like.

When we have negative feelings about our bodies, we tend to avoid thinking about them or focusing on them at all, aside from the times when we are judging them. Most of us don't actively engage in paying attention to our bodies because it results in feeling shame, sadness, and disgust. These feelings then typically spiral into thoughts about how big our thighs are, if our breasts are too saggy, or if our hip bones are too pointy and sharp-looking. But what could happen if we started to utilize mindfulness in terms of how we approach our bodies? Remember that nonjudgmental part of mindfulness? What if we could just simply observe our bodies as they are without judgment? Seem impossible? Maybe. I'm not saying it's easy. I am guilty of avoiding this most of the time! It's often just too painful to really let myself know and be with my body as it is. But I'm curious how you feel this could benefit you. This is a good opportunity if you would like to take a pause from reading to reflect and journal about what you are feeling and thinking right now. What would it feel like to sit with and tune into your body and push away those judgmental thoughts? How might your relationship with your body begin to change?

Poor body image contributes to a lack of mindfulness during sex as it manifests in distracting cognitions, unpleasant emotions, and avoidant behaviors during sex. A perfect example of this is being overwhelmed with thoughts and worries about a particular body part to the point where you try to hide that body part from your partner(s). It's nearly impossible to be in the moment and focused on your body and any pleasurable sensations you might be experiencing if this is happening. And it's so common! I can't tell you the number of clients I've had over the years who have reported this kind of problem with sex, but it's a lot. It's not just my clients, either. I have had similar experiences myself. Maybe on that particular day, I'm feeling self-conscious about the cellulite on my behind. I will be so focused on how to "hide" this from my partner that I'm not at all mindful or able to enjoy what is happening. And I put the word hide in quotation marks because let's face it – we all know that we aren't really hiding anything – but we sure do try!

It might feel scary to even think about being more present during sex, and that is okay! You might be thinking to yourself, "Why would I want to bring attention to my body when I really don't like my body?" That's totally fair. It takes a lot of vulnerability to switch your focus from literally everything else in the world to what is happening in your body when you're not particularly happy with your body. Let's practice some non-judging here and try not to label yourself as "bad" or "wrong" for having these thoughts and feelings. Instead, let's allow this as another opportunity for curiosity, this time more specifically around how your judgmental thoughts about your body impact your ability to enjoy sex. Pull out that journal again, or just think about the following questions.

> Have you ever found yourself shut down during sex because of your negative thoughts about your body?
>
> Have you moved your partner(s)'s hand away from a part of your body you didn't like?
>
> Have you hidden a part of your body as I have with the cellulite on my behind?
>
> How do you think hiding or diverting things from your partner(s) impacts your ability to experience pleasure?
>
> How might that change if you were able to let those thoughts go? Identify some goals for yourself of how you would like to use mindfulness to let go of body negativity to improve your sexual experiences.

One of the easiest ways to start practicing mindfulness is to start paying attention to what is happening around you in the present moment. Use your five senses to observe what is around you. What do you see, smell, feel, taste, hear? Take a moment to notice any thoughts or feelings that come up about what you are observing. Chances are that some other random thoughts will come into your mind as you practice this, but that is totally okay and is to be expected! Simply acknowledge them and let them go: "There you are, pesky, annoying thought about my dinner date tonight. I'm not going to think about that now. Please move along." You can practice this exercise anytime, anywhere, and for as much or as little time as you would like. If you are new to mindfulness, I'd encourage you to start practicing for a few minutes a few times a day just to get used to the feeling of being in the moment and letting thoughts go.

Five Senses Sensual Mindfulness Exercise

We can even expand these mindful observations in a more sensual and erotic way. Here is an example of how to practice this. I invite you to give it a try.

For this exercise, you will want to give yourself at least 15-30 minutes of time in a quiet space. Ideally, this will be in your bedroom so that you can get comfy and cozy in your bed, but any place where you can be alone and relax will work just fine. Take some time to prepare the space by considering your idea of a sensual environment. Some possibilities are to dim the lights, light some candles, play some soft music, change into lingerie, have your favorite lotion or essential oil handy, pour yourself a glass of wine, and maybe prep yourself a bowl of strawberries with whipped cream. If you'd like, you can include a vibrator or other sex toy in the experience. This all sounds sensual and romantic to me – but think about what might feel good to you. The objective is to create an opportunity for you to tune into your senses in a way that you might not normally do for yourself.

Step 1: Take a few minutes to sit quietly and tune into your body. Take a few relaxing, deep breaths, noticing the air as it passes through your nose and mouth. Allow yourself to notice any thoughts that might pop in and gently acknowledge them before letting them pass by. Be gentle and remind yourself it's okay to have thoughts as you choose to let them go.

Step 2: Shift your focus to your sense of sight. Use your eyes to look around. Notice colors, changes in light, textures, and movement. If you have a candle lit, what effect does the flickering light have on your environment? Look at a picture on the wall or notice the edge of the bed, the ceiling, the details of lingerie you might be wearing, or any food or drink you brought into the experience. Pay attention to your surroundings and look for things you have not noticed before. Bring in a sense of nonjudging by simply paying attention and not assigning meaning to anything you are looking at. Try to use objective, fact-based terms to describe what you are seeing. For example, the "berries are red," not "the berries look juicy and delicious."

Step 3: Gradually shift your focus from your sense of sight to your sense of sound. Close your eyes and notice all the things you can hear. Is there music playing? Can you hear sounds from outdoors or elsewhere in your home? Be mindful of any sounds that come your way, letting them go in one ear and out the other.

Step 4: Now, shift your concentration to noticing the smells of your environment. If you have essential oils or lotions nearby, this is a great time to open them. Without dispensing them from their bottles, take time to simply smell them and focus on the aromas. Are you able to pick out specific layers of scent? Mindfully breathe in the other scents around you – the sheets, the air, your skin. If you have a beverage or food, what does that smell like? Take your time to really take in the smells of your environment.

Step 5: Gently shift your focus to your sense of taste. If you've brought in some food or beverage, take your time to really taste, noticing the flavors and intensity. Sip your drink slowly, savoring the taste. Take small bites of your food. Focus on any texture you feel in your mouth and how your mouth responds to the food. Do you start to salivate a bit? Does your mouth pucker? Consider flavors of sweet, sour, bitter, etc. Resist the urge to judge the food and drink as good or bad. Simply notice how your taste buds respond.

Step 6: Focus now on your sense of touch. Grab your lotion or oil and squeeze a bit into your hands. Notice the feelings and sensations that this creates on your skin. Pay attention to the pressure between your body and where you are sitting or lying. If you are in bed, do the sheets feel soft? Run your hands along your clothing or skin. What does it feel like? Run your fingertips gently up the inside of your arm. Feel the air across your skin. Maybe you have a feather nearby or an ice cube from your beverage. Run those items along your skin and notice the different sensations. If you have chosen to integrate a sex toy or vibrator into your experience, this is the opportunity to use it. Try not to assign a judgment of whether something feels good or bad. Simply notice how it feels.

Step 7: When you are finished with the exercise, take a deep, full breath. Pause and take a moment for gratitude and acknowledge your remarkable body that allows you to see, hear, smell, taste, and touch.

Since mindfulness is a practice, I encourage you to use this exercise as often as you can. The great thing about the exercise is that it can really be adapted in so many ways, and it creates an opportunity for endless experiences depending on the environment you create and the objects you include. If you have a safe, private outdoor area, it creates an entirely different atmosphere, allowing for sounds such as birds chirping, sights like flowers or the sky, all kinds of smells, and sensations such as breeze, sunshine, and grass. Plus, being outdoors allows for a mindful connection with nature, which brings all sorts of other benefits. The exercise is also easily adaptable for use with a partner or partners. The limits with this one only end with your imagination.

Body Scan

Now that you can practice mindfully tuning into your surroundings let's move that awareness to your body. Body scans are an excellent way to cultivate a connection with our bodies in a non-threatening, hands-off kind of way. There is an abundance of body scan scripts on the internet and on meditation apps. The one provided here is a little different in that it includes specific parts of the body that are traditionally thought of as being sexually sensitive, such as genitals and breasts. It also encourages the use of sensual reflection and observation of other body parts, as just about any part of your body can generate sexual excitement. As with the five senses exercise, work to bring a gentle curiosity to this practice and try to let go of unwanted thoughts and judgments. I would recommend giving yourself at least twenty minutes in a quiet setting to get the most out of the body scan.

Step 1: Take a deep breath and close your eyes. Slowly and deeply breathe in and out, pushing away any thoughts that come into your mind. Let go of noises or distractions that may be happening around you.

Step 2: After a few minutes of focusing on your breath, slowly bring your attention to your toes. You may want to wiggle your toes a bit if you can, noticing how that feels. If you are wearing socks or shoes, pay attention to how that feels. Simply notice without any judgment what is going on with each individual toe, the space between them, and the point of contact between the toes and your footwear, the floor, the air, or whatever they are touching. Take note of any sensations you feel while focusing on your toes. As you focus on your toes and their sensations, consider how it might feel for them to be touched. Imagine yourself or a partner(s) touching your toes in various ways, and take note of any sensations or desires that arise. Do not judge these sensations or desires. Simply observe them.

Step 3: After a few minutes of focusing on your toes, move your attention and focus to the rest of your feet. Pay attention to the sensations of your feet in the same way that you did for your toes. Imagine your feet being touched, and take note of any desires or sensations that this brings up.

Step 4: Slowly shift your focus up your legs in the same way you did for your toes and feet. Notice the sensations in your ankles, calves, knees, and thighs. Can you feel your legs on the chair or bed, pressing against whatever you may be sitting or lying upon? Consider how they might feel to be touched.

Step 5: Slowly shift your focus to your pelvis and pubic area, including your genitals, while you continue your gentle exploration into sensations and desires that you notice here. Pay particular attention to what it might feel like to be touched in these areas. Again, let go of any judgments that arise. This exercise is simply for you to observe your body as it is at this moment. You might not feel anything at all in certain body parts, or the thought of touching them or having them touched might not evoke anything for you. That is okay – tune into the sensation of not feeling anything.

Step 6: Continue the scan throughout the rest of your body: your stomach and lower back. Your chest, breasts, and mid-back. Your upper back, shoulders, and chest. Your neck, head, and each part of your face – nose, mouth, eyes, ears. Finish the scan down your arms and into your fingers. Pay particular attention to your breath and its impact on your bodily sensations as you move through your abdomen and chest areas. If your mind begins to wander during this exercise, gently notice this without judgment and bring your mind back to the sensations in whichever part of your body you are at. If you become aware of any discomfort, pain, or stiffness, do not judge this. Just simply notice it. The same goes for any scars, wrinkles, rolls, or dimples you may feel. Do not judge; simply notice. Observe how all sensations rise and fall, shift and change from moment to moment. Pay attention to how no sensation is permanent. Just observe and allow the sensations to be in the moment, just as they are. As you scan each individual area, ask yourself how it might feel for that area to be touched by a partner or by yourself in a sensual way.

Step 7: As you have now scanned each individual area of your body and observed its sensations, take a few moments to observe your body as a whole. Use the same gentle curiosity and push away any unwanted thoughts or judgments.

Step 8: Return your attention to the present and take a moment for the gratitude of your body and all its sensations and desires.

This body scan exercise can be practiced as often as you would like. The intention is not for relaxation but for awareness; however, I have had a lot of clients report relaxation as a side effect, making this a great exercise to try before bed.

Four Dimensions of Touch for Individuals

Most of us would agree that touch is essential to a romantic or sexual relationship with another person. I also believe it is essential in creating an improved relationship with ourselves and our bodies and an excellent way to practice mindfulness. The five dimensions of touch is a couple's exercise developed by sex therapist Barry McCarthy to help couples who are struggling with intimacy[3]. I've adapted this concept to four dimensions of solo touch and am offering it to you here as a mindfulness tool that you can use to connect to your body in an incremental way.

The focus of this exercise is to utilize touch as a mindfulness tool. You will move through each dimension of touch gradually and at the speed that works best for you and where you are in your relationship with your body. There is no right or wrong way to use the dimensions. You might start at dimension one and stay there for a day or for a year, or you might use them in no particular order – practicing dimension three one day, dimension one the next day, and dimension four the following week. The goal is to simply use these exercises to work on getting to know your body in a nonjudgmental and loving way.

Dimension One: Affectionate Touch— Affectionate touch is not sexual or sensual. It is a way of showing affection or caring. It usually involves clothes-on touching. One great way to give yourself affectionate touch is with a butterfly hug: crisscross your arms with palms towards your chest, hooking your thumbs together, and patting yourself gently on the chest. You can also show yourself affectionate touch by wrapping yourself in a cozy blanket or using a weighted blanket.

Dimension Two: Sensual touch— This involves non-genital pleasuring, which can be clothed, semi-clothed, or nude. Sensual touch with self might include a hand or foot rub. Try running your hands up and down and along various body parts. Explore different types of pressure and touch – what differences do you notice between stroking, rubbing, and squeezing?

Dimension Three - Playful touch – This dimension integrates genital touch with non-genital touch and can be clothed, semi-clothed, or nude. One idea for playful touch is to touch yourself in the shower or bath (try using the shower head or water-based lube to make the touch even more playful). Another playful touch experience is to throw yourself a sexy dance party for one - turn up your favorite sexy music and dance around the house as you run your hands up and down your body and through your hair.

Dimension Four: Erotic touch —this dimension is mostly focused on genital touch but might also include non-genital touch as well. You can participate semi-clothed or nude. The goal is to generate sexual and erotic sensations in the body by using your hands. If you have an orgasm, great, but this is not the intent of dimension four.

The wonderful thing about the individual dimensions of touch exercises is that they allow us a safe space to practice being mindful without the pressure that might come from being with a partner or partners. It acknowledges and addresses the vulnerability of being with our bodies in a mindful and non-judging way. During and after participating in the dimensions of touch, ask yourself: How does this feel both physically and emotionally? Was there any part of touching myself this way that felt surprising? How might I share what I've learned with my partner(s), and how might it help me with being more mindful during sex? By utilizing these four dimensions of touch, hopefully, you will start to engage with your body in a mindful way that allows for you to slowly bring that practice into partnered interactions.

Summing It Up

Mindfulness is being in the moment in a non-judgmental way.

Challenges to being mindful include our own constant thoughts and the messaging that tells us to multitask in order to be effective.

Being mindful can help us to focus on our bodies in ways that minimize judgment of them.

Being mindful can help with sexual pleasure by focusing on the sensations we are experiencing at that moment.

A lack of mindfulness takes away from our ability to connect to ourselves and our partner(s).

There are several exercises that can help us practice mindfulness, including using our five senses, body scans, and touch exercises.

CHAPTER TWO

Connecting – Becoming One with Ourselves and Others

So far, in Chapter One, we have learned about mindfulness – what it is and how to use a variety of exercises to be more mindful. One aspect of mindfulness is its effectiveness in creating a space for connection. This will be helpful as we now move into Chapter Two and focus more on how to connect not only with our partner(s) but with ourselves.

As humans, we are social creatures. We not only crave love and belonging, but according to Maslow, it is one of our essential human needs. Kleinplatz and her colleagues found in their research that connection, alignment, merger, and being in synch were one of the important factors in attaining great sex. When we first think of connection, we might automatically think that this has to do with our relationship with our partner(s). However, participants in the study reported that self-acceptance was also essential in creating the level of connection necessary for positive sexual encounters. The way women feel about their bodies is an important aspect of self-acceptance and fits with what we are working to improve in this book.

Using Values to Connect to Yourself

One way to work on building that connection with yourself is through engaging in solo activities that you find energizing or calming. The activity can be just about anything that you like to do: walking in nature, petting your dog or cat, creating art, listening to your favorite music, or cooking dinner. But these activities are even more effective at building self-connection if they align with your values. Values are essentially the core beliefs that define what is important to you. We can engage in an activity, but if it doesn't align with our values, we aren't going to get the maximum benefit from it in terms of connecting with ourselves. However, suppose we are mindful of our values when we decide what activities to engage in. In that case, we will automatically strengthen our self-connection by being true to ourselves and what is most important to us. For example, one of my key values is nature. This means when I choose to engage in activity that integrates nature – whether that is pulling weeds in my garden, going for a hike, or just sitting next to the creek on my parent's property – I'm connecting with myself in a much deeper way than I am when I do something like watch TV. That doesn't mean I can't continue to watch and enjoy TV – it just means that I am aware that watching TV doesn't allow me to connect to myself in a meaningful way because it doesn't align with any of my top values.

I have provided a list of values below. I am going to encourage you to go ahead and write in your book and circle the values that are the most important to you. If you are a person who would rather not write in the book, that's okay – just grab a notebook or your journal and make a list of the ones that you find important. There are many more possibilities, so if something comes to mind that is a value of yours but is not listed here, please include it in your list. While identifying your values, try to dismiss anything that the messaging you have received from outside sources like society, family, or friends might have told you that is "supposed" to be important to you. As you read each value, consider what that value means to you. In other words, how do you define this value and the importance of the value to you - not how important you think it should be or how important you have been told it is.

An example is success. Over the years, I've had a few clients work on this values identification exercise and discover that success isn't nearly as important to them as they'd been told it "should" be from others. Once they had this realization and were able to identify the values that truly resonated with them, they were able to make healthy changes to their life and a few more connected to themselves.

Power/Influence	Courage/Risk Taking	Balance	Creativity	Curiosity
Efficiency	Faith	Success	Knowledge	Truth
Family	Wealth	Teaching/ Mentoring	Patience	Friends
Fame	Equality	Dependability	Love	Altruism
Generosity	Gratitude	Self-Respect	Sustainability	Adaptability/ Flexibility
Support	Nature	Independence	Fairness	Integrity

Frugality	Uniqueness	Attentiveness	Empathy	Toughness
Determination	Integrity	Compassion	Humility	Loyalty
Tolerance	Peace	Beauty	Wisdom	Adventure
Solitude	Connection	Learning	Self-Reliance	Fun

Now that you have taken a moment to consider and identify your values, consider what kinds of activities might align with each one. Here are a few examples to get your ideas flowing:

Grab a book and head to a coffee shop for some uninterrupted reading – aligns with solitude and knowledge

Start a vegetable garden – aligns with nature, sustainability, and self-reliance

Do a jigsaw puzzle – aligns with determination and fun

Spend an hour or two at a local arcade – aligns with fun

Meditate – aligns with spirituality and solitude

Give yourself a manicure and/or pedicure – aligns with beauty and self-reliance

Bodily Awareness

We will shift gears now and focus on a different kind of awareness and connection with self. Sadly, many women lack understanding or knowledge of their bodies. One study of 171 adult women found that when shown a diagram of the external female genitalia, only about 9% could identify all the anatomy, with only 41% able to correctly identify the vagina[4]! I am guessing these numbers would be even lower if the study focused only on women with body image issues since chances are we are not spending much time looking in the mirror or getting to know our genitals if we don't feel great about our bodies in general. Especially since the messaging tells us that vulvas are supposed to look a certain way, and if we know or suspect ours doesn't look that way, we will feel bad about it. There are a few problems with this message. One is how can you connect with yourself if you do not have this basic knowledge of your bodily anatomy? Another is that there is no right or wrong way for a vulva to look. Each one is as completely unique and different as the woman who owns it. This is demonstrated beautifully by the Labia Library – a project that shows the wonderful diversity of women's genitals. I have provided the link in Appendix D and encourage you to have a look. Once we can see our bodies – including our genitals – exactly how they are and not how we think they should be, we can more easily connect to them and allow ourselves to experience pleasure.

The classic way to get to know your genitals is to grab a mirror and take a look, which we will get to in a moment. But before you get the mirror, take a moment to study the following images. The first one is an external view of the female genitals or the vulva[5]. Most people confuse the vulva with the vagina when in fact, the vagina is on the inside of your body while the vulva is the collection of organs that you can see from the outside. I love how this diagram is very mechanical, as it does not insinuate that the vulva or any of its parts have to look or be a certain way. It simply lays them all out in a very nonspecific but easily comprehensible way. In the diagram, you'll see the outer lips or labia majora, the inner lips or labia minora, the vestibule or area between the labia minora, the urethral opening, and the vaginal opening. You'll also see the clitoral hood and clitoris.

The description of "inner" and "outer" describing the labia can be deceptive because the labia minora can extend out of the labia majora, or they can be tucked away inside. Neither way is normal nor abnormal and is just an example of how different each set of genitals can be. Coloring can also be different. Some labia are uniformly colored, or they might have an ombre look to them, gradually darkening towards the tips. The labia majora can also have a wide variety of appearances – from puffy to more flush with the body. Again, all presentations are normal and beautiful in their own unique way.

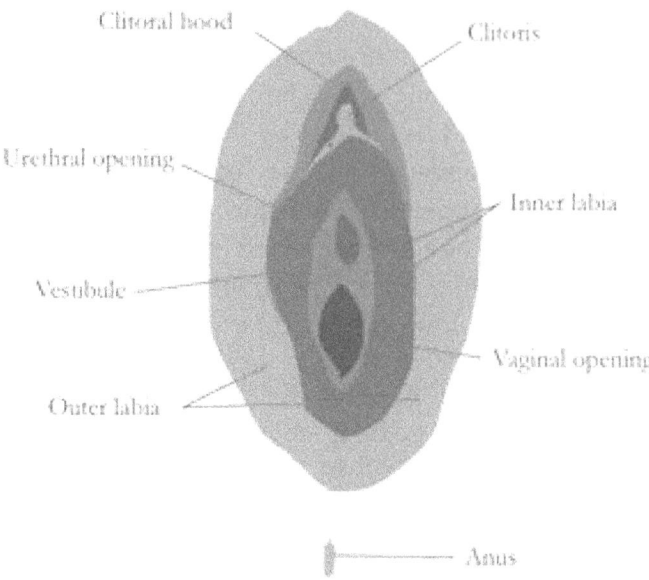

Next up is a more detailed diagram of just the clitoris, which is important to review, even though during your mirror exercise, you won't be able to see the whole thing[6]. This is because there is a lot of misinformation and a lack of understanding about the clitoris. It's much more than just a "magic button" or nub at the top of the vulva. That "nub" part is the glans, which is about the size of a pea and is loaded with nerves that account for how sensitive it is. The clitoris also consists of a pair of crura or "legs" and vestibular bulbs that run internally within the tissue of the vulva, straddling the urethra and vagina. Like the penis, the crura and bulbs fill with blood when aroused, increasing sensation in the vaginal canal.

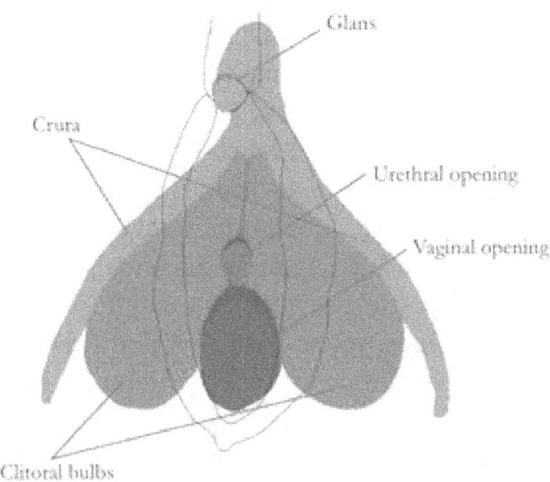

Now that you've had time to study the images and learn a little about the pieces and parts, it's time for the mirror. This can be a scary exercise for many women – especially if your genitals are a part of your body that you have some negative feelings towards. So, let's build on the nonjudgment that we learned in Chapter One and bring some of that to this experience. Take some time, as you prepare to look at your genitals, to think about any specific beliefs, feelings, or concerns that you have about them. In what ways has the messaging influenced how you feel about your genitals? Gently acknowledge those thoughts and feelings and push them away. If you need to, this is a good opportunity for journaling and exploring your thoughts, feelings, and their origins.

Next, find a position in which you can do this exercise comfortably. That might be squatting on the floor with the mirror between your feet, sitting on the edge of the chair with your legs apart and the mirror between them, or any other position that works best for you. You may want to use a flashlight aimed at either your genitals or the mirror. I also recommend using a small amount of lube on your fingers to make it a little easier to navigate the labia so you can fully investigate and get to know yourself.

Once you are in a comfortable position where you can see yourself well in the mirror, take some time to nonjudgmentally observe the vulva and what it looks like. Feel the different parts, spreading the labia majora and minora, touching the clitoral hood glans, and running a finger around or even inside the rim of your vaginal opening. As you observe the different parts of your genitals, remember to practice being mindful and nonjudgmental, observing in a purely objective way. If you experience any painful or negative thoughts during the experience, remind yourself that it is not only okay but helpful to explore and know your body. You can also kindly acknowledge the thoughts and push them away. Once you feel satisfied with your exploration, pause for a moment of gratitude for your genitals and for what they do for you.

Another great way to cultivate body awareness and build a connection with yourself if you are a woman who menstruates is to track your cycle. If you don't already do this, you can use an app or an old-fashioned paper calendar. This type of awareness can help with learning to listen to your body and what it is telling you. It can help you make decisions throughout the month based on what your body needs, and it can be a great way to practice tuning in and listening to how your body feels and why it feels that way. "Oh, I'm having cramps. It must be because I'm a few days from starting my period," or in my case, "I could literally eat the house today. I am so hungry; it must be I'm getting my period in ten days."

Interestingly, a small 2013 study in the journal *Perceptual & Motor Skills* revealed that **during menstruation, women tend to perceive their body size as larger than it really is**[7]. Despite there being no real difference in their size, forty-four women in the study were more likely to choose larger body images to represent themselves during their period. If you are a woman who menstruates, by tracking your cycle, you can be aware of this potential bias and utilize self-compassion skills to respond accordingly.

Setting Boundaries with the Messaging

An important part of connecting with yourself, as we mentioned earlier, is knowing yourself. One of the biggest and most obvious issues I have seen in working with clients with poor body image is that most information used to make decisions about their bodies comes from external sources. It can be challenging to know yourself and what you really want when you are bombarded daily with the messaging. The messaging is literally everywhere, telling us what we are supposed to look like, how to feel, and if we don't look or feel like that, what to buy so we can. It comes from movies, TV, music, and social media. It also comes from sources closer to us, like family and friends. But what if we just said "no" to the messaging? What if we started to limit our exposure to the messaging? What if we set out to find different messaging? What if we made intentional choices around the products we buy?

You can start to do this by using mindfulness to pay attention to how you feel throughout the day. When you notice a negative body image thought or feeling, pause to ask yourself what is triggering that experience and set boundaries accordingly. For example, a client recently shared with me that she decided to start online dating again after taking a few months to focus on herself when her last relationship ended. She noticed that when she was selecting photos to include on her profile, she started to experience negative body image thoughts and feelings. "I started really giving into the negative self-talk of my stomach looking fat in one photo or me having a double chin in another photo. It really didn't feel good to not want to show my authentic self to people who I would potentially be dating." Ultimately, she decided that she was going to choose photos she liked that represented how she truly looked and not ones that hid certain aspects of her body or that were taken at "good angles." This client didn't realize it at the time. Still, she was doing a great job of setting boundaries with the messaging by not listening or giving in to the negative self-talk, saying that her body wasn't good enough in certain photos or that she had to look a specific way to participate in online dating.

These boundaries can look however we need them to. It might mean asking a friend or relative to stop complimenting you when they think you "look skinny" in a certain outfit. It might mean actively deciding not to renew your Weight Watchers subscription. It might mean purchasing some bright red lipstick you like simply because you like it and NOT because you saw it advertised in a magazine. It might mean wearing the crop top you love, even if it shows your stomach.

This isn't just about what we cut out of our lives. It can also look like taking an active role in selecting the things we allow in. For example, what do you think could happen if you actively followed body and sex-positive influencers on social media? What if you could find even just one influencer out there who looked like you, and you focused on listening to that voice and that messaging while you worked to shut out all the rest? You can! You have the ability to curate your social media feed in a way that makes you feel good instead of bad! No matter how well we think we can resist the urge to compare ourselves, there are certain pages and sites that are going to make us feel bad about ourselves. We are human. Start by looking at the accounts you are currently following and ask yourself how they make you feel. Do they make you feel bad about yourself? Unfollow them. Do they make you feel empowered? Make sure to like their posts so that more of them show up in your feed.

Social media has been a blessing and a curse, but one great aspect of it, especially in the last several years, is that it is a wonderful way to find those people who look like us. Whether you are a woman of color, aging, queer, disabled, muscular, fat, androgynous, femme, or whatever you look like, chances are you will be able to find someone out there who looks like you and is not afraid to show themselves to the world. Try searching for various descriptors or tags, find and follow these people, like their posts, and regularly be on the lookout for more like them. This type of representation can truly be empowering.

Building Connection with Partner(s)

Because sex isn't just about what is going on within us but also about what is going on between ourselves and our partner(s), we are going to take some time now to focus on building connection with them. Sometimes, we are so lost in what is going on with ourselves, for example, worrying about what our bodies look like, that during sex, we struggle to pay attention to what is going on with our partner(s). The problem with this isn't just that our partner(s) may lose out on pleasure, but we do too! How can we give feedback or ask for what we need if we are too focused on what is going on with ourselves and have no idea what our partner(s) is doing or feeling? We will learn more about communication and how to make those asks a little later in Chapter Four, but for now, we will focus on building that base of connection that will make communication easier.

Allowing Partner(s) to Love You as You are

So often, our partner(s) want to love us just the way we are, but we get in the way. Sadly, we sabotage our experience of receiving love because of how we feel about our bodies. Why in the world would we do this? It will probably be no surprise at this point that it is partly due to the messaging. We learn over time that we are not worthy of love because of our flawed bodies. And so, we put up walls. We dismiss compliments that our partner(s) give us. We hide our bodies from them. We don't let them touch us. We create distance. In essence, we destroy connection and create a hostile environment where it makes it impossible to even exist.

My wife once said something to me that broke my heart. I was going on one of my typical rants about how much I hated my body, how ugly I was, and how horrible I looked on that given day. She very quietly and calmly looked at me and said, "I wish you wouldn't talk about the person I love like that." Those words stopped me in my tracks. It had never even occurred to me what it must be like for her to hear me saying those things to myself and about myself. It had simply become one of my coping skills. I said those things out loud to protect myself from anyone else's negative feedback. I was trying to beat them to the punch. The really twisted part of this, though, is that the person I was saying it in front of, my loving wife, would have never in a million years said or thought those things about me. Whenever I find myself falling into that behavior again, I remind myself of her words, and I stop. I might not always be able to replace those negative thoughts with positive ones, but at least I stop them and stop talking trash about the person she loves. You might even want to engage your partner(s) in helping you with this at first. Ask them to hold you accountable by pointing out gently when you start talking negatively about the person they love.

The thing that is so profoundly sad to me about us not allowing our partner(s) to love us is that we are deserving of love. We were born deserving of it, and the way our body looks should not stop us from receiving it. I have a feeling that if you were to think back to your child self, you would agree that they deserve to grow up and be loved regardless of what they look like. This is a quick and easy exercise that can help reinforce that in a visual way. Find an old photo of yourself as a child. Look at the photo and repeat this mantra or one similar: *"I deserve to be loved and accepted in this exact body. I will no longer entertain people or messages that tell me otherwise." Put the photo in a place where you will see it regularly, and each time you do, repeat the mantra to yourself, reminding yourself that you are deserving of love as you are.*

Learn Your Love Languages

Love languages are something that you may have heard of. In fact, you might already know both your and your partner(s)'s love language. If you don't, I've included a link in Appendix D to the online quiz – it's quick and easy, and I recommend you and your partner(s) take a few minutes to take it. I will not go into detail about each of the different love languages here, as the book about them by Gary Chapman provides an excellent explanation. Rather, I explain why they are a tool that can help build a connection with your partner(s). The five love languages are quality time, acts of service, words of affirmation, physical touch, and gifts, and a recent study showed that sexual satisfaction was elevated in relationships where partner(s) expressed love in the way the other partner(s) preferred to receive it[8]. The book does a wonderful job of describing each of these in detail, but they are essentially what they sound like. For example, my love language is physical touch – this means both giving and receiving touch, which does not have to be sexual in nature. My wife's love language is words of affirmation. She loves to hear that she did a great job at something, to be thanked for something she did, or to be complimented. It isn't a problem if, like us, your love language doesn't match your partner(s)'s. The problem is when we don't have an awareness of our love languages. The lack of awareness can cause resentment or disconnection. But when we are aware of our own and our partner(s)'s love language, we can do a better job fostering connection by doing the things that we know they need or by asking for the things we need in order to feel loved and appreciated in the relationship.

Summing It Up

Connection is an important part of a satisfying sex life. It is equally important to connect with yourself and your partner(s).

The messaging that we receive throughout our lives from society, family, and friends often interferes with our ability to connect with ourselves. It can help to get to know your values and to set boundaries with the messaging.

Getting to know your body, your genitals, and your cycle are great ways to connect with yourself.

We are allowed to and need to set boundaries with the messaging in order to strengthen our connection with ourselves.

Actively curating our social media intake is an important way of setting boundaries with the messaging.

Body image issues often get in the way of us having a truly meaningful connection with our partner(s).

We need to actively choose to let our partners love us as we are in order to build connection.

Learning our and our partner(s)' love languages can help to build connection through understanding.

CHAPTER THREE

Intimacy – Getting Close to Yourself to Get Closer to Others

In Chapter Two, we dove into connection. Not only the connection with our partner(s) but the connection we have with ourselves. We explored the importance of connection as it relates to body image and sex and learned how the messaging from society, family, and friends can interfere with true, meaningful connections. Exercises were provided to assist with tuning out that messaging and to learn how to make stronger connections with self and partner(s). In this chapter, we will focus on intimacy, which often flows much more naturally when we have built a strong connection.

Intimacy is a common word that comes to mind when we think about sex and what makes sex good, so it comes as no surprise that it is one of the factors identified in the research of Peggy Kleinplatz and her colleagues. Specifically, they found that participants reported that intimacy required genuine respect, caring, acceptance, and admiration in order to create a sense of trust. Sadly, the words in that description – "genuine respect, caring, acceptance, and admiration" are not the words that come to mind when I think of someone struggling with body image issues and how they think and feel about themselves. In fact, I believe it's more of the opposite. Things like believing we are flawed and unworthy of acceptance and belonging come to mind. I think of a lack of caring and a lack of admiration for self. These are all part of the experience of shame. As Brené Brown defines it, shame is "an intensely painful feeling or experience of believing we are flawed and therefore unworthy of acceptance and belonging."[9] Based on this definition, it would be reasonable to expect that someone experiencing shame would have a hard time with intimacy. Our tasks in this chapter will center around dismantling shame and building shame resilience so that you can start to allow yourself to feel accepted - not only by your partner(s) but by yourself as well.

Self Compassion

Self-compassion is the practice of treating yourself with a nonjudgmental understanding and kindness. It also requires a realization that pain and struggle are part of the universal human experience.

Self-compassion is a helpful tool to use in fighting against the impacts of any negative body image or inadequacies that we might feel. A very common and easy self-compassion exercise is to start talking to yourself the way that you would talk to a friend. I know that I would never tell a friend that I think her thighs are disgusting or that her cellulite is offensive, yet I tell these things to myself on a practically daily basis. The next time you notice yourself being critical of your body, stop and consider if you would say these things to a friend and challenge yourself to find something kinder to say instead. It does not even necessarily have to be related to the original criticism if that is too hard to challenge right now. Just try to find something kind you can say to yourself or something positive you can feel good about. For example, I might have a critical thought about how wide my hips are, and I might not be able to find a way to have kindness towards my hips – but I can shift my thinking away from my hips and tell myself that I am proud of getting my progress notes done before leaving the office today.

Another way to consider self-compassion regarding that statement about my hips is to focus on what my hips *do* for me versus how they look. I could think about how my hips provide a strong foundation for my legs, allowing me to walk independently. Admittedly, this form of self-compassion comes from an ableist mindset, as I recognize that women with disabilities might not be able to easily focus on what their bodies can do without it bringing up more body shame. If this is the case for you because of a disability (or for any other reason), I would encourage the use of acceptance in conjunction with self-compassion.

Acceptance is tricky – when I even just mention the word to clients, it often brings up a sense of dread or annoyance. There seems to be a belief that by accepting something, we are giving up or not trying. I challenge this by offering a different point of view. Acceptance isn't giving up. Rather, acceptance is a very intentional process that requires us to make active choices. It acknowledges that we will not always love our bodies or even like them. It acknowledges that we will not always love the way our bodies look or feel or how they move (or don't move). Acceptance is what happens when we are willing to acknowledge these things and say, "That's okay." It means we aren't letting those concerns hold us back from things like amazing sex. It means we are actively choosing that, despite how we feel about our bodies, we will find ways to live our best lives. Of course, I understand that acceptance, like many of the things discussed in this book, is not easy. It's also not a place we just arrive at and stay. Some days, acceptance is easier than others. But it starts by making a choice to be kinder and less critical by using self-compassion, the other tools in this chapter, and the book as a whole.

Name the Shame

It is no secret to those who know me that I'm a huge Brené Brown fan. Her research around shame and the effects of shame has been life-changing for me and many of my clients. According to Brené, the ability to "speak shame" is a critical part of dismantling shame and breaking free of the impact it has on our day-to-day lives[10]. When we don't speak up and identify our shame, its source, and its impact, we internalize it. We keep it a secret, and it eats away at us. It contributes to feelings of powerlessness, hopelessness, and isolation – and these are certainly not the ingredients for intimacy.

For this name-the-shame exercise, you are going to want to grab a journal or notebook. We are also going to take a few minutes to prepare for the possible emotions that will arise. Shame is something that runs incredibly deep for most women – especially body shame. Because of how intense this emotion can be, I want you to take a few deep breaths and prepare your space in a way that feels cozy and safe. Maybe that is dimming the lights, lighting a candle, using aroma therapy, snuggling up to a pet, or wrapping yourself in a fuzzy blanket. Once you are feeling safe and secure, start thinking about the parts of your body for which you feel the most shame.

It might be painful, but try to be very real with yourself about how you feel about these body parts – or even your body as a whole. Write down some of the thoughts that you have about your body that cause the most shame. Include how the body parts might contribute to sexual shame, and be specific. Some examples might be:

My labia are weird-looking, and I don't want my partner(s) to see them.

I hate when my partner(s) sees my belly (or hips, or saggy boobs, or thighs, or any other body part) during sex.

I hate how my protruding hip bones poke my partner(s), making me self-conscious and wondering if they wish I had more curves.

I don't want my partner(s) to touch my mastectomy scars (or caesarian or any other scar).

I think my vagina smells/tastes bad, so I avoid letting my partner(s) give oral sex.

My skin issues make it difficult for me to let my partner(s) touch me because of the pain and itchiness.

I can't move like I want to in order to feel or be sexy.

I hate having to think about taking off my prosthetic or keeping it on during sex.

I lost weight, but now I have saggy extra skin, which is gross and gets in the way when we try to be intimate.

The next step is to read this list out loud. You can read it to yourself, but even better would be to read it to someone in your life whom you trust. Maybe it's a friend, partner(s), or your therapist. It doesn't matter who it is, but it must be someone with whom you feel safe enough to be vulnerable to name your shame. And that's it! You did it! Take some time to reflect on how it felt to get those shame-inducing thoughts out of your head, onto paper, and spoken out loud. They don't live alone in your head anymore. Hopefully, this will make it easier to work on the rest of the exercises in this chapter, which are designed to help you build empathy, self-acceptance, and self-love.

Forgiving

Let's talk about forgiveness. You have probably heard the saying "letting someone live rent-free in your head"? Well, this is what happens when we are unable to forgive. Think for a moment about a person or people who said or did something that contributed to your body image in a negative way. Now, think about what might have caused that person to do or say what they did. Is it possible to cultivate some empathy for that person? Are you able to come to an understanding that maybe they were exposed to messages about beauty standards that contributed to how they acted towards you? Maybe they didn't have coping skills that would have helped them to understand how toxic those messages are. Maybe they were projecting their own shame and self-hatred onto you. We won't know for sure necessarily, but can we try to at least look at the situation from a different lens? And if we can, does that help with forgiveness? When we go along with the belief that people say or do things that hurt us out of malice, it is much harder to forgive them, which makes complete sense! Who wants to forgive someone who hurts us purposely? But when we can start to put ourselves in their shoes or have empathy for them, we can start to let go and move on. We are not necessarily letting them off the hook or saying that what they did was okay, but we are looking at that person as human and realizing that maybe they were doing the best they could at that moment. Cultivating empathy for others can help us to have empathy for ourselves. And why is that important? Because empathy is the enemy of shame. And it can also help us forgive ourselves.

It is important for us to not only work to forgive others but also to forgive ourselves. What do we need to forgive ourselves for? I mean, after all, aren't we just the victims of external forces that came together to create this horrible, negative body image we have? Aren't we just doing the best we can in a world full of messaging that is constantly telling us we aren't good enough? Yes, these things may be true, but here is an example from my life that might help illustrate the importance of forgiving ourselves:

I have recently noticed myself feeling full of regret and anger when I think of how my younger self ate like garbage and did not exercise regularly. I get caught up in thoughts like, "Why didn't I just create healthier habits 20 years ago?" I blame her so much for where I am today in terms of my weight, my health, and my body image. Now, that is a lot of rent-free space that younger me is taking up in my head today. But what would it be like for me to forgive her? To come to an understanding that she was doing the best that she could? To realize that she didn't necessarily have great role models for eating healthy and exercising and that there were lots of factors in her life at the time that contributed to her behaviors? I think it would help me to let go of that anger and regret and be more mindfully aware of the things that I can control and change TODAY. Can you work to do this for yourself? Think about the things you blame yourself for and try to cultivate some empathy and understanding by using this formula:

> I forgive myself for _____. I am letting go of the pain and shame that I feel due to this. I am accepting that I am human and that humans make mistakes. I would likely make a different choice today, but I was doing the best I could at the time.

Stop Judging Others

When we are taught the societal messaging to shame ourselves, we are, by default, taught to shame and judge others as well. Interestingly, research tells us that we often judge people in the same areas in which we are vulnerable to shame and that we do so as a type of defense mechanism to make our own shame more bearable. For example, if I judge someone else's body or sexuality, even if just for a moment, I will feel less shame about my own. The problem is that when you criticize another person's body, you reinforce the belief that bodies are a measure of a person's value. This is what makes developing empathy such an important aspect of dismantling our own shame.

Before we dive in more deeply about learning how to cultivate empathy for others, let's get clear on what empathy is. Empathy is often confused with sympathy, but the two are very different. Brené defines empathy as "listening, holding space, withholding judgment, emotionally connecting, and communicating 'you are not alone.'"[10] Sympathy is pity, an "I feel sorry for you" emotion. It doesn't require us to really get in the trenches with the other person or allow them space to be vulnerable with us. Here is an example of a sympathetic versus an emotional response to a friend who is feeling shame about gaining back some weight she had previously lost:

Sympathetic response: I'm sorry to hear that. Don't worry, I'm sure you can lose weight again - since you did it before, you already know you can do it.

Empathetic response: I'm sorry that you gained the weight back. I know how hard you worked to lose it and how happy you were. I can hear how frustrated and upset you are now.

I want to emphasize here that judging others does not make us bad people. It makes us humans who are susceptible to the messages we receive. Judging can even be a great instinctual coping skill. It helps us to make snap decisions in the moment that can keep us safe. So please, don't beat yourself up for being judgmental of others. What you can do, though, is to start being more aware of your judgments. When you find yourself shaming someone, you can pause and ask yourself where the judgment is coming from. Is it something we truly believe? Or is it coming from the messaging? Once you realize that judgment is intrinsic, you can focus on empathy. Put yourself in their shoes for a moment. Get curious and consider if there are reasons for their situation.

Learning to do this with our judgments towards others and being empathetic towards them can help us to do it with our self-judgments as well. We can learn to turn that empathy inward and listen, hold space, and connect with ourselves. We can tell ourselves, "You are not alone." We can examine our judgments and ask ourselves what their origins are. We can come to a true understanding that both we and others deserve more compassion and empathy and less judgment.

Name the Love

We "Named the Shame" earlier in this chapter, so now we are going to try something a little different. This exercise is best done in front of a mirror, but I know that it can be scary or even impossible for some women. This can particularly be challenging for those with certain disabilities or visual impairments and for trans women for whom looking in a mirror might cause dysphoria. So, if you are unable to use the mirror at first or at all, that is totally okay. You can still do this exercise by imagining your body, looking at it without the mirror, or looking at only the parts of your body in the mirror that you are comfortable viewing rather than looking at the whole thing.

While standing in front of the mirror (naked if you feel comfortable) or while imagining your body, write down some of the things or parts about your body that you love. I realize this might not be easy. The things we don't like about ourselves often flow from our brains so much easier than the things we like. It is ok to start small. Maybe it's your hands, ankles, eyes, shoulders, or hair that you love. Maybe it's your fingernails or your eyelashes. It doesn't matter how small or insignificant the body part feels – if you love it, write it down. Now, consider how you might be able to emphasize this body part. For example, if I choose my fingernails as the body part that I love, I might emphasize them by getting or giving myself manicures on a regular basis.

The next step, just like with naming the shame, is to read your list out loud. Again, you can read it to yourself, but even better would be to read it to someone in your life whom you trust – ideally, the same person you shared your shame with. Unlike the shame exercise, this one isn't a one-and-done. I would encourage you to review and update your list at least once a week. If you weren't comfortable in front of the mirror the first time or being naked, try to move towards that as a goal. Also, challenge yourself to add at least one item each time. Think outside the box. Maybe you don't love the way your thighs look – maybe they were even on your shame list – but maybe you love the way they feel when you wrap them around your partner(s).

Write that down! The more you do this exercise, the more you will cultivate a genuine admiration for your body.

Find the Kid in You

Because external factors so heavily influence shame, it can be helpful to remind ourselves that there was a point in history when we once loved our bodies. We were not born hating our rolls or our jiggles. Children do not inherently feel shame or feel bad about themselves. In fact, they are often in awe and excited about their bodies and their various parts. Have you ever seen a toddler groove to music? Have you ever seen kids running gleefully with no destination or reason? Do you remember chasing fireflies and splashing in mud puddles? Dipping your fingers into a paint pot and smearing it all over the paper? Playing with slime or Play-Doh? Did you ever choose a fun, colorful outfit and wear it out of the house without the slightest care in the world of what others would think? These are all bodily ways in which we allowed ourselves to feel joy as a child that we often deny as adults.

Now, take a moment to reflect and focus on a time when you felt joyful in your body. You may have to go way back – but what was that time? What were you doing? Tapping into that emotion and working to generate it intentionally can be a powerful way to work at dismantling shame. I asked a client recently to name a time that she felt joyful. She teared up a bit as she remembered a time from her childhood when she would skip down the street hand in hand with her best friend after school. I then asked her what it might feel like for her to skip today as an adult. She grinned and got excited. But then shame peeked through and started to hold her back. She started to worry about what others might think or how her fat might jiggle as she skipped. By the end of the session, though, she had agreed to skip in her driveway three times before her next session. Three times might not seem like a lot – but it did two things for this client. It gave her a starting point that felt do-able. And more importantly, it created a base from which she could start building other joyful bodily experiences. When she came to her next session, she was excited to share with me that she had been skipping every day to her mailbox and that she was even thinking about other things that might bring her body joy, such as dancing or swimming – both of which were things she hadn't done in years due to shame.

Dress Your Body Affectionately

Sometimes, when we are feeling insecure about our bodies, we consciously or subconsciously put on clothes meant to cover up as much of our body's "trouble areas" as possible or to attract the least amount of attention. The problem with this is that it reinforces messages of shame and negativity. By doing this, we are buying into the belief that only certain body types are worthy of wearing certain articles of clothing. But who says that bikinis or crop tops or short shorts were only made for certain body types? We need to challenge that by wearing the clothes that we like and that make us feel good. This means being intentional and expressing your personality and wearing what you like – not what you think will look good. You can also do this slowly if it feels more comfortable by starting with a new top in a bold color or even an accessory like a scarf or earrings that feel more representative of you and your personality than what you might typically wear. When we dress our body intentionally, we are treating it as something that's worthy of attention and love. We send the message—to others and to ourselves—that this is a body that is loved and worthy of beautiful things.

This is also a great exercise to practice erotically. Buy some lingerie that you would not normally buy because of how it exposes a part of your body you don't feel good about. Again, if this is something that makes you feel uncomfortable, start small. You don't have to wear the lingerie in front of your partner(s); you can wear it alone. Or you can even wear a robe or comfy pj's on top of it until it feels more comfortable. The point is to start allowing yourself to wear things because you like them and because you want to.

Learn the Facts

To come to an understanding and acceptance of ourselves that will allow us to experience true sexual intimacy, it is important to be knowledgeable about any misinformation that may inform our feelings of shame and inadequacy. I could write volumes of educational material about both sexual satisfaction and body image, but I will focus here on the common misconceptions that relate to both bodies and sexual shame. In the appendices, you will find suggested sources if you would like to expand your knowledge further.

Myth	Fact
"Vaginal dryness is bad"	This happens sometimes at all ages and stages. There are many variables that contribute to vaginal dryness, none of which reflect on your body or your partner(s)'s ability to turn you on.
"Pubic hair is gross."	The fact of the matter is that pubic hair is, well, just pubic hair. It's not necessarily gross or appealing – it's just a personal preference around how you'd like to groom this area. Having hair down there actually has some benefits. It reduces friction and skin irritation, helps regulate body temperatures, and reduces the amount of sweat produced around the vagina, and it helps protect the vagina from bacteria related to STIs, UTIs, and yeast infections.[12]
"Nipples should be a certain size."	Nipples, like labia, are a unique part of your body. Some are small and pointy; some are larger and flat. Some are inverted. Some don't match. It's all ok!
"My labia are the wrong color compared to my other skin."	Labia come in a range of hues, from pink to purple to brown or black, all of which are completely natural and normal. It is common for the labia to be a shade darker than the rest of your skin, especially for black women.
"My vagina is too loose" or "My vagina is too tight."	Vaginal tightness changes over a woman's lifetime and may sometimes feel too tight or too loose, depending on certain factors. The vagina is designed to have sex and birth a baby, but these events, along with aging, can change the tightness, elasticity, and shape of the vagina.

Summing It Up

Intimacy is a component of great sex.

Intimacy requires genuine respect, caring, acceptance, and admiration to create a sense of trust.

Shame is the enemy of intimacy because it prevents us from respecting, admiring, and caring for ourselves in the way that we deserve.

Naming the shame is the first step in dismantling shame.

Naming the love is a great way to bring in positive messages about your body.

Forgiving self and others can be a powerful way to let go of shame and judgment.

Exercises like Find the Kid in You and Dress Your Body Affectionately can help cultivate self-compassion, reduce shame, and therefore create space for us to find intimacy.

Knowledge is power! Knowing the true facts about sex and bodies can help us to let go of false information that might contribute to self-judgments that get in the way of intimacy.

CHAPTER FOUR

Communication – Let's Talk About Sex...and Bodies

In the last chapter, we did a lot of challenging (but hopefully rewarding work) around intimacy as it relates to body image and sexual satisfaction. We confronted shame and embraced love. We learned about the importance of forgiveness and challenged some myths about bodies and sex. We're now going to take the next step forward and talk about communication.

Kleinplatz and colleagues identified in their research that a complete and total sharing of self was essential for a satisfying sex life. Communication is one of the crucial tools that we can use to accomplish this sharing. Communication is also how we learn to cultivate empathy, another tool that helps with the dismantling of shame around body image and sexual self-schemas, as discussed in Chapter Three. The obvious thing that comes to mind for most people when they think about communication is how we interact and share information with others. This is certainly important for our goal of reducing body shame and increasing sexual satisfaction, but equally important is our ability to communicate with ourselves. Consider, for a moment, what is the nature of the conversations you have with yourself. I'm guessing if you are reading a book about body image, the conversations aren't great. The good news is you *are* reading a book about body image and taking steps to improve those conversations with yourself.

Sadly, in my practice, I see that both types of communication are something that many people struggle with on a day-to-day basis – and not just when it comes to sex. Communicating effectively and vulnerably with others and ourselves is just something we aren't really taught how to do. Instead, much of how we learn to communicate with ourselves and others is informed by watching the communication style of unhealthy people, leading to unintentionally replicating those patterns.

When it comes to sex, the struggle with communication is even more evident. This makes sense when we consider the shame and embarrassment around bodies and sexual desires. It can be hard to share a desire or fantasy with your partner(s) if you've learned somewhere along the way that it was wrong or bad. This is further complicated by feeling unworthy due to body image issues. But communication is so important. Improved communication with our partner(s) can allow us to hear what they love about us and our bodies and that pleasure (theirs and ours) does not have to be limited by our body size, looks, etc. Applying more positive communication with ourselves can help to reduce shame and improve overall mental health, allowing easier communication with others. Because of these benefits, this chapter will focus on exercises aimed at learning different techniques that will help improve communication not only with our partner(s) but also with ourselves.

Positive Self-Talk

Positive self-talk is a practice that can feel strange and awkward. This is something that always makes me sad because negative self-talk is a practice that, for many people, doesn't feel strange but actually feels normal and perfectly okay to engage in. Before we jump into learning how to engage in more *positive* self-talk, let's explore the origin of your *negative* self-talk. Negative self-talk comes from our inner critic and often exists as a defense mechanism. A defense mechanism is an unconscious response developed by the brain to protect us from unpleasant thoughts or events. They are meant to be helpful. I know it sounds a little twisted to think of negative self-talk like that but bear with me for a minute. Remember the messaging? All of the things we experience on a daily basis that tell us how we are supposed to look and feel. Picture a busy highway. On one side of the highway are all of those "shoulds" that come from the messaging and our past experiences. On the other side of the highway is you. The inner critic is the crossing guard that directs the traffic between the you and the "shoulds." Maybe it recognized how you felt increasingly sad and discouraged when you saw that your body didn't match images of what the world considered sexy, and so it started using criticism as a form of motivation and a way to help get you across that highway from where you were to where you thought you were supposed to be. The problem is that this isn't actually helpful because of the fine line between motivation and self-punishment.

Take some time to consider your inner critic. First, let's give it a name. This is helpful because it separates it from you and makes it easier to challenge negative self-talk. You are not the one with the negative thoughts about you – it is. Next, get to know it a little. What kinds of things does it have to say? Why do you think it is saying those things – is it trying to let you know of an unaddressed need? Do you remember when it first started saying them? Can you think of a time when it was helpful? If so, thank it for that, but then set a boundary with it by reminding it that you don't need that kind of help anymore. Going forward, whenever you experience negative self-talk, remind yourself that it is the critic talking and do what you need to do to address it without submitting to her. This could look like thanking it for showing up again, asking it to leave, or acknowledging that it is encouraging you to address a need that you are neglecting.

While learning how to deal directly with the inner critic is important, talking kindly to yourself is an important part of challenging the inner critic. Think of a recent situation in which you were self-critical due to making a mistake. How did you feel in that situation? Ask yourself if you are the only one who has ever made that type of mistake. How do you know this? Have you seen a friend or family member in a situation like this? Consider for a moment what you would say (or what you did say) to a friend or family member who made a similar mistake. Now, give that same kindness to yourself.

Now that you've learned how to deal with your inner critic in a compassionate way, we're going to work on generating some positive self-talk by developing a mantra. A mantra is a positive statement that you say to yourself either silently or out loud to encourage and motivate yourself. You could easily go online and find hundreds, if not thousands, of examples of mantras. But I don't want you to do that. In my experience, a mantra can only be helpful if it is something that you develop yourself and believe to have elements of truth. The mantra cannot help you if you don't believe it or if it doesn't feel personal. At the same time, for the mantra to be most effective, it should also be a bit audacious. It should challenge you a bit and make you feel a little uncomfortable.

Creating a mantra can be challenging. To make this a little easier for you, here is a list of questions to consider and an example of a mantra that might make sense for each:

What compliments or positive statements have I received but been unable to see as true? Can I rework these to feel more honest to me?

> Sample mantra: *My curves and my body are worthy of the love that my partner(s) have for them.*

What part of my body do I feel the most shame about? What might I be able to say to that body part if I was free of that shame?

> Sample mantra: *My worth isn't dependent on the size or shape of my belly.*

What parts of my body do I already love? How does this body part make me feel? Can I apply this feeling or description to my body as a whole?

> Sample mantra: *My entire body deserves the love and respect I feel for my legs.*

What would you like to say to your body if you were to consider everything it does for you? What do you think your body would like to say to you?

> Sample mantra: *My body is a gift, and I appreciate the way that it loves me despite the pain I experience at times.*

Once you have settled on a mantra that feels comfortable but also just a little uncomfortable, make it a point to say it to yourself a few times each day. You can also integrate your mantra into any mindfulness or meditation practices you do. I like to encourage clients to write their mantras on Post-it notes and stick them on their mirrors and other places where they will see them throughout the day.

Another way that I encourage clients to generate positive self-talk is a practice that I call internal gratitude. Internal gratitude requires giving yourself credit daily. Instead of focusing on the things you messed up, did not get done, or don't feel good about, challenge yourself to identify three things that you did well that day. It doesn't have to be anything major like solving world peace; for me, sometimes my internal gratitude consists of giving myself credit for doing the dishes. I hate doing the dishes! By giving yourself credit every day, you will train your brain to look for positives, instill self-compassion, and even find the motivation to accomplish more.

Self-Touch

Touch is one of the primary ways we communicate nonverbally, not only with others but with ourselves. It is especially powerful at conveying emotions like love and empathy – two emotions that we know are important for improving our body image and creating connection. One powerful form of self-touch is masturbation. Despite some messaging that solo sex is wrong or shameful, it is an excellent way to get in touch with your body and create a tangible reminder of the pleasure that our bodies can provide. When you allow yourself to regularly experience orgasmic pleasure and the rush of dopamine, endorphins, and oxytocin that accompany it, your body innately becomes easier to love and accept as it is. It does not matter what your body shape or size is, how old you are, what race you are, or how you identify; you are worthy of and able to experience pleasure right now as you are. However, I do want to note that things such as gender dysphoria and sexual trauma can make masturbation more challenging. If this is true for you, it's ok. There are other areas of your body that you can touch and derive pleasure from, such as your lips, chest, inner thigh, and neck. This isn't limited - all bodies are different – explore your body to see what feels good for you!

Some clients have told me that they don't masturbate because they don't like it or can't orgasm from it. I like to challenge those clients a little bit to think outside their comfort zone and consider other ways in which they might be able to masturbate that would be more pleasurable. Getting in different positions, using lube, or even water play in the shower can be enjoyable ways to engage in solo pleasure play. Using erotic literature or porn can also help make masturbation more enjoyable. There are even apps with recorded erotica, and a lot of erotic fiction can be found in audiobook form.

Sex toys are also a great option for use in masturbation. If you aren't familiar with sex toys or find them intimidating, I've listed a few sources in Appendix D of sites that make it easy and fun to shop. Something to keep in mind when it comes to buying sex toys is to look in the middle when you start out. By this, I mean avoid the cheapest but also the most expensive toys. The least expensive will often break quickly, not function properly, or be made from a material that is not easily cleaned. On the other end of the spectrum, the most expensive may not always be the best value. There are so many different toys out there, and because different people enjoy different things, start out by trying a variety of moderately priced items. Once you figure out what you enjoy the most, you can invest in more expensive products if you desire.

I also challenge clients to prioritize giving themselves pleasure without worrying about whether an orgasm will or won't happen, and they are often surprised at how much more enjoyable masturbation can be. Sometimes, they even end up having an orgasm once they get out of their heads and let go of the performance anxiety, as it isn't something that only happens with your partner(s)!

Oxytocin, an anti-stress chemical that has been linked to overall well-being, has been found to be released by activation of sensory nerves during sex; however, self-touch does not have to be sexual or sensual to be beneficial. One study found that low-intensity stimulation of the skin that occurs through touch, such as light strokes, also releases oxytocin[13]. I believe that in addition to these benefits, touching ourselves in a loving way can help us connect to our bodies and accept them as they are.

Self-touch can feel a little awkward or strange at first if you aren't used to it. One exercise that I often teach clients as an easy way to start practicing self-touch is the butterfly hug that we learned in Chapter One. As a refresher, to give yourself a butterfly hug, crisscross your arms with palms towards your chest, hooking your thumbs together, and patting yourself gently on the chest. You can also wrap your arms all the way around yourself and give yourself a big bear hug. Other ways to practice loving self-touch are:

Gently stroke your cheeks with the back of your hand

Rub your fingernails gently up and down your arm

Place a hand over your heart or chest and feel your heartbeat or your breath rise and fall

Massage your thighs, calves, or feet

Asking For Validation

There is this popular saying that I'm sure you've heard: "You can't love someone else until you love yourself." To me, this is problematic for a few reasons. Don't get me wrong, there's some truth to it – obviously, self-love is important – but to think that we can't love others or be in a loving relationship until we achieve some master level of self-love is a pretty extreme viewpoint that can end up holding people back from connection to others. In fact, I believe that we learn a lot about how to love ourselves by the way that others love us and that we would miss out on this completely if we waited around to enter a loving relationship until we love ourselves first.

Seeking external validation may seem contraindicated in a book to help you to improve your body image. "How is asking my partner(s) to tell me that I'm sexy going to make me feel sexy?" That's a legit question, but validation and compliments are some of the ways that love is expressed, so being able to ask for validation is an important part of communication in a healthy relationship. This can also help combat shame around body image and negative sexual schemas, and it models how to give ourselves validation by being open to receiving validation from our partner(s). However, the key is to understand that while it is okay to desire and request validation, it is only one component of many that contribute to our overall well-being and, therefore, cannot be the only source of what helps you to feel good about yourself. Similarly, self-validation cannot be the only source of what helps you feel good. I believe the best thing is a balance between self and external validation – and this goes for other things beyond bodies and sex, too!

Asking for validation can feel awkward regardless of how well you and your partner(s) communicate, how long you have been together, or how comfortable you feel with them. I encourage clients to break down difficult conversations into three steps:

1. Give a brief and objective description of what is happening: "I'm really struggling today with my body image. I feel like my butt is huge."

2. State how this is making you feel: "It makes me feel shame about myself overall and doesn't make me feel sexy or want to have sex."

3. Ask for the validation: "Can you please let me know what it is you like about my butt? It would really help to hear that from you right now."

This very simple process is direct and to the point. I love it for this purpose of asking for validation, but it can also be easily adapted for many other issues that you might be having in your relationship or life that require assertiveness – such as setting boundaries, which we will be discussing next.

Boundaries

How many times have you been with a friend or group of friends and found everyone in the conversation falling into reinforcing negative thoughts about bodies? Maybe you are out to dinner, and as you are all deciding what to eat, one person says something like, "Ohhh the burger sounds amazing, but I didn't work out today, so I better not." And then this starts a spiral of responses: "Yeah, I need to lose weight for my friend's wedding, I should just have the salad," "If I eat dessert, I will have to do a double workout tomorrow," and on and on. Even if you arrived at the restaurant not thinking negatively about your body, you are pretty much guaranteed to do so if this is what you're hearing around the table. It also reinforces diet culture messaging around what kinds of foods are "good" and "bad" and frames exercise and movement as something that we need to do in order to minimize feelings of guilt or justify behaviors.

It's pretty easy to see why conversations and comments like that can be damaging to our body image, but what about compliments? Things like "How much weight have you lost? You look great!" or "You are so lucky to have a butt like that – it looks great in those jeans!" can be equally as damaging to our body image as they emphasize the belief that bodies are something that we should judge.

So, what is the best way to handle these situations? Boundaries. Boundaries are those lines that we set with others to let them know what is okay and what is not okay. Setting boundaries can be helpful as they are not only about drawing a line, but they are also a way of communicating to yourself what is important to you. When we set a boundary, the person we are setting it with may not honor it, but we can still feel good knowing that we know ourselves enough to recognize what is important to ask for and that we have the confidence to ask it.

An example of a boundary that might work in the example of dinner out with friends is to say something right when you sit at the table, such as "Hey everyone, I'm really working on my body image issues, and comments around food can be triggering for me, so I would really appreciate it if we could just order our meals without comments about the food. I'm really here to see you all anyway, not to focus on what I'm eating." And the compliments? A simple "I'd rather not talk about my body" or "I'm focusing more on my health right now" can do the trick.

Part of setting boundaries includes how we talk in general about bodies. Try using mindfulness to observe your language for a day or two. One word that can be problematic is "fat." While it has recently been reframed as a descriptor of body size rather than an insult, it can still be a source of shame for many people. It is also problematic as it tends to be used as a "feelings word" – for example, saying "I feel fat." Instead of saying that, try to tune into your body and be more accurate about how you are feeling. Is it that you feel full? Unattractive? Uncomfortable?

Words that might seem more acceptable, like "curvy," "thick," or "big-boned," still reinforce the judgment of bodies, especially when they are used to describe someone in a negative way. Overweight and obese may also feel less judgmental; however, they are problematic in that they frame weight as something that should be within a certain range, and they tend to have a health-related association when health is not related to a person's weight or size. Instead of these words, try people at higher/lower weights, people with more/less weight, and people with larger/smaller bodies.

The way that we talk around and to others also matters and is a way to reinforce and model our boundaries. Don't engage in judgmental talk around food at the dinner table. Compliment friends and loved ones on their non-weight/non-body related achievements and personality traits.

Sensate Touch

As mentioned earlier in the chapter, touch can be a powerful form of non-verbal communication. When we expand touch away from self-touch to touch with a partner(s), we are allowing for the complete and total sharing of self that Kleinplatz's research participants talked about being essential for great sex. This can be done using sensate exercises. Sensate techniques can help people with body image issues learn to be more connected to their sexual pleasure because they are based on the goal of touching without any judgment, expectation, or evaluation. The focus in sensate touch is specifically on sensations that allow you to let go of any distractions or worries around your body. Through sensate focus, you can learn that you are capable of sexual response and pleasure regardless of what your body looks like. Sensate focus, while primarily centered around touch, can also include verbal feedback about what types of touch are pleasurable or not. Here, I provide a simple version for engaging in sensate touch with your partner(s). Try to designate at least 15-30 uninterrupted minutes for the exercise.

Step One: Set boundaries and expectations by discussing with your partner(s) any body parts that you would like to remain off-limits to touch in this exercise.

Step Two: Get in a comfortable position and take off as much clothing as you feel comfortable removing. This is not an exercise designed to result in intercourse but rather is focused on communication through the receiving of touch and the providing of feedback.

Step Two: Allow your partner(s) to give physical touch in all areas of the body that were designated as acceptable in step one. The touch does not have to be sexual. Try using different pressures and parts of the hand and fingers – for example, lightly using fingertips versus deeper pressure with full palm and hand. Refrain from "massaging" or purposely touching for sexual pleasure. Give feedback in real time to your partner(s). Try to be specific about what feels good and what does not.

Step Three: Take some time to debrief. Consider what sensations and types of touch felt most pleasurable and which did not.

Other Touch Exercises

Touch does not have to be sensate or sensual to help us connect and communicate with our partner(s). Try lying next to each other on your backs, hold hands, and close your eyes. Then, place your other hand on your partner(s)'s abdomen, with theirs on yours. Feel their abdomen rise and fall, and allow your breathing to naturally synchronize. This can bring a sense of closeness and intimacy that can even allow for verbal communication by making it easier to have meaningful or difficult conversations. Other ways that touch can bring us closer to our partner(s) is by bathing each other, spooning or cuddling, dancing, or hugging. When engaging in these activities, focus on what your partner(s)'s touch is telling you and what you are conveying to them through your touch.

Summing it Up

Communication is a tool that can help achieve complete and total sharing of self, one of the components of good sex.

Your inner critic originated out of a place of good intentions. Name it, understand it, and set boundaries with it.

Positive self-talk is an important way to practice healthy communication with yourself.

Positive self-touch is a daily practice that can help us know our bodies and judge them less.

It's okay to ask for validation from our partner(s) – it doesn't mean we don't love ourselves. In fact, it is even okay to be in a healthy relationship and not fully love yourself.

We can and should implement boundaries around conversations that make us feel bad about our bodies and sex.

Touch exercises with our partner(s) – both sensate and others – can be meaningful ways to connect and share ourselves with them.

CHAPTER FIVE

Authenticity – Be Yourself, Be Yourself!

In Chapter Four, we learned a lot about communication and how important effective, healthy communication with ourselves and our partner(s) is to improving our body image and having more satisfying sex. We explored our inner critics, which are often a source of unhealthy internal communication, and learned ways to deal more effectively with those critics. We learned about verbal and non-verbal communication, and several exercises were offered to help with both styles of communication. Learning how to communicate effectively with ourselves and our partner(s) is important before moving into what we will discuss in this chapter – authenticity – because as you learn about your authentic self, you will already have the tools you need to express this authenticity in your relationships and with yourself.

Another component of great sex, according to the individuals that Kleinplatz and her colleagues interviewed in their study, is authenticity, genuineness, and being wholly oneself. When I think about how this applies to body image and sexual satisfaction, it feels essential to me that for us to be completely ourselves, we need to shed the core beliefs that contribute to our shame and find who we are underneath all of that. This will require devoting time to identifying and processing our thoughts and the impact they have on our emotions and reactions – specifically our behaviors around sex. The process involves recognizing that something is not working, acknowledging that it needs to change, and having the willingness to take steps toward that change. We need to be able to embrace our inherent perspectives and beliefs and let go of the world's perspective and what everyone else is telling us to believe. In her book, *The Body is Not an Apology*, Sonya Renee Taylor encourages readers to consider how they would act if they didn't listen to or believe the "outside voice" or the voice that tells us we aren't good enough (the messaging). When we were born and throughout early childhood, we did not have feelings of unworthiness. We loved our bodies and were intrigued by them. We were not aware of the outside voice. But over time, the outside voice became louder. We started to question ourselves and our bodies because the outside voice said there was something wrong with us. We start to forget about our true inside voice and start to mistake the outside voice for our own. In this chapter, we will dig into and learn about what informed our core beliefs, how these beliefs may have held us back from being our true authentic selves, and discover ways to start challenging those beliefs. I will warn you: this work is not easy. I encourage you to make your space safe while you work on these exercises and refer to the grounding techniques in Appendix A as needed.

Origins of Our Beliefs

To change, we must first know where we are currently, in the here and now. We do this by gaining an understanding of where our thoughts, feelings, and behaviors originate from and what influences them – because, as the 1960s feminist slogan stated - the personal is political. The messaging related to body image can be either positive or negative and can originate from society/media, family, and friends. These messages inform us of what an ideal body is and how to attain it. The most basic example of the messaging is that the ideal woman is: "young, tall, thin, and White, with at least moderately large breasts" and that by purchasing weight loss supplements, anti-aging creams, plastic surgery, makeup, etc., we can achieve this ideal[14]. Of course, this ideal body may vary a bit. For example, Asian women may have heard an outside voice encouraging a petite and school girlish appearance, while Latina individuals have been told by the messaging to value a "curvy" body with large breasts, rounded butts, and a generally "thick" body shape. For disabled women, the voice likely tells them that there is no ideal body image that fits them and that they are not capable of being sexy or sexual beings. Rather, they are viewed as asexual, undesirable, or even helpless due to their disability. Lesbians who choose to present in a more masculine way may feel pressure to feminize their appearance because of the messaging around what women "should" do regarding hairstyles and clothing choices.

Regardless of the exact message, the results can be devastating. In 2010, the Girl Scouts Research Institute conducted a national survey of girls aged 13-17 and found that nearly half (48%) of the respondents "wished they were as skinny as the models they saw in fashion magazines," and 47% said fashion magazines gave them a body image to strive for. AOL.com and The Today Show conducted a similar survey in 2014, which found that 80% of teen girls compared themselves to images of celebrities, and almost half of that group stated the images made them feel unhappy with their looks[15]. Worrying about bodily things such as cellulite, fat, breast size, stomach, or other body parts, and the appearance or smell of genitals can then reduce sexual satisfaction.

Not only does messaging have an impact on how we feel about our bodies in general, but it also has an impact on how we feel about our bodies in terms of our sexuality. Consider for a moment what kind of education you had around sex growing up. Who taught you? What did you learn? Most girls do not learn much beyond the basics related to menstruation and pregnancy, and even that learning can be misinformed. When conversations around women's bodies and pleasure are not prioritized or when the conversations are tainted with misinformation or unrealistic expectations, we learn that these things are either not important or that we place a standard of performance on ourselves that cannot be attained. Messaging around women's bodies and sexuality does not come solely from porn as one might expect - exposure to rom-com movies, television shows of all genres, books, magazines, and social media – can all lead women to judge their bodies, sexual functioning, and experiences as inadequate.

Media influence on body image can be so impactful that a 1994 study by Stice & Shaw showed that only three minutes of exposure to ultra-thin models significantly increased body dissatisfaction[16]. Messaging from parents that informs body image can include not only comments made about how one should dress, one's weight, or one's eating habits but also more subtle messaging. For example, how a mother feels about her own body and a daughter's awareness of her mother's dieting can negatively impact body image[17]. Teasing from peers and discussions with friends around dieting and body shape or size also influences an individual's body image.

Let's take a moment to consider what informed your beliefs about your body and your sexuality. This will help to start separating the outside voice from your own internal voice. The example provided here is brief, but take time to go through and think about all the different sources and messages you have received over the years – and maybe even still receive. If the space here isn't adequate or you prefer not to write in the book, use your journal.

EXAMPLE	Media/Society	Family	Friends
Body Image	Seeing thin, beautiful models in music videos	Family members making judgments of women in larger bodies	Being teased for developing early and having curves
Sex	Romantic movies that showed sex was always hot and steamy	Sex was something that wasn't discussed in a serious way	Being sexual or interested in sex made me a "slut"

	Media/Society	Family	Friends
Body Image			
Sex			

Identifying and Challenging Your Cognitive Distortions

Now that you have been able to take some time to investigate the messaging that contributes to your thoughts and feelings around body image and sex, we're going to dive into the specific thoughts themselves and work on challenging them so that they have less of an impact on our sexual behaviors. We all experience faulty thinking or cognitive distortions. It doesn't mean there is something "wrong" with us. It just means we are human. One thing that I like to remind clients of is that we can't control our thoughts. Our brain just makes them up all the time. But what we can control is how we choose to respond to them.

Cognitive Behavioral Therapy (CBT) is an intervention that I like to use with clients to help challenge their cognitive distortions. Cognitive distortions are the faulty thinking patterns that we habitually fall into and are often inaccurate and negatively based. CBT is based on the premise that our thoughts impact our emotions, which then impact our behaviors. However, this isn't necessarily a linear process. Our behaviors can also impact our emotions, which impact our thoughts. Here is a diagram that helps visualize how this works:

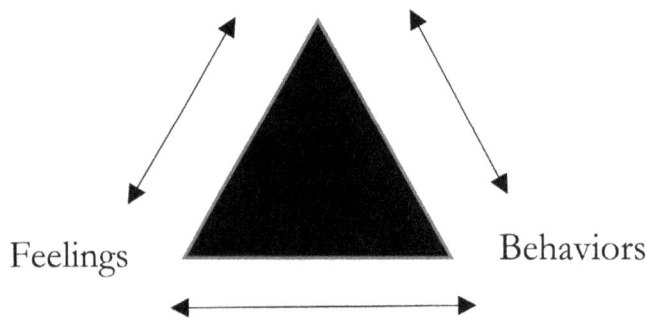

An example of this is when I experience a thought about how disgusting my stomach looks. This causes feelings of shame and sadness, which then causes me to avoid letting my partner(s) see my stomach or to avoid sex altogether. This behavior then leads to feelings of disconnect from my partner(s) and more sadness or feelings of awkwardness around sex, both of which could lead to thoughts that my relationship is doomed or that my partner(s) hates me. You can see how this can easily become a vicious cycle that we can get trapped in.

One of the first steps in dismantling our cognitive distortions is being aware of them. Part of this awareness comes from being able to recognize not only the thought itself but also the impact it has on our feelings and our behaviors. Using the example I provided above for guidance, try to recall a recent distressing thought, how it made you feel, and the resulting behavior:

Thought		Feeling		Behavior

Now, let's work on challenging the thought. There are several questions you can ask yourself to do this:

What is the evidence *for* this thought?

What is the evidence *against* this thought?

Is the thought based on opinion or facts?

Is this thought helping me in any way?

Are there other less polarizing ways to think about the situation or myself?

Am I making assumptions?

Would I think this about a friend?

Is there someone with whom I can check the facts around this thought?

Am I holding myself to a standard that I set or that the outside voice/messaging set?

Finally, is there a replacement thought that is more realistic that I can use in place of this thought?

Now that you have had a chance to challenge the thought let's use this chart again to see how the replacement thought can make a difference in our feelings and behaviors. I have provided an example of how I was able to replace the initial thought of "My stomach is disgusting" and the resulting change in feelings and behaviors.

Thought	→	Feeling	→	Behavior
I'm not happy with the way my stomach looks. But that is okay. Everyone feels like that sometimes. How I feel about my appearance does not determine my worth as a partner.		Neutrality		No negative or positive change in behavior- which is okay since I'm not avoiding sex or hiding my body from my partner.
Thought		Feeling		Behavior

As I mentioned earlier in the chapter, this can be hard work. How did it feel completing this exercise? Do you think it will be easy or difficult to work on challenging your thoughts? Don't worry if this doesn't come naturally. Change is difficult, and often, we are working to change and challenge years and years and years of faulty thinking that is reinforced daily by the messaging that comes from society, family, and friends. It might be discouraging to hear this, but I'm going to be honest. I'm not sure that we can ever completely stop experiencing negative thoughts about our bodies. How can that be a realistic or reasonable expectation for us when we live in a world where these messages are constantly raining down on us? Even with the biggest umbrella we can find, in a downpour, we are still going to get a little wet. I tell you this not to take away your hope but to help you manage your expectations and to encourage you to be kinder to yourself. When you continue to experience negative thoughts about your body, remember it is the outside voices – the messaging – informing those thoughts, not your internal voice. You are not broken for having body image issues. You are simply a human product of the world we live in.

Understanding Your Identity

Part of being yourself is *knowing* yourself. We all have multiple aspects of our identity, and our identity impacts how we see our bodies and how we feel about them. Our body image and our sexuality can be part of our identity. Some research has indicated that certain aspects of our identity – particularly those which we experience distress about - are correlated to body image issues[18]. The identities that we tend to feel distressed about are the ones that are marginalized or oppressed. For example, as women, we are a marginalized identity, and so simply by virtue of being a woman, we will have some sort of body image issues. The more marginalized identities you have, the more body image issues you are susceptible to. So, as you can see, our identity impacts and is impacted by both things we are striving to improve in this book.

There are two main categories under which aspects of identity fall – personal and social. Aspects of personal identity are what make you different from others. This includes the things that define you as an individual and what make you who you are. Characteristics of our personal identity may involve career, hobbies, favorite things, aspects of personality, and the roles we have, such as an only child, big sister, mother, daughter, etc. Some aspects of my personal identity are reading as a hobby, working as a sex therapist, purple as my favorite color, being an only child, and being introverted as a personality trait.

Social identity is about how you identify yourself in relation to others. In other words, it is the identity you share with similar group members. Some examples of this would be religion, disability status, sexual orientation, race, class, and age. Aspects of my social identity are being age 45, queer, white, and able-bodied.

Using the grids provided on the next couple of pages, identify different aspects of your personal and social identities. Place a star (*) by any identities that are privileged and the letter "A" - by any that are marginalized or oppressed.

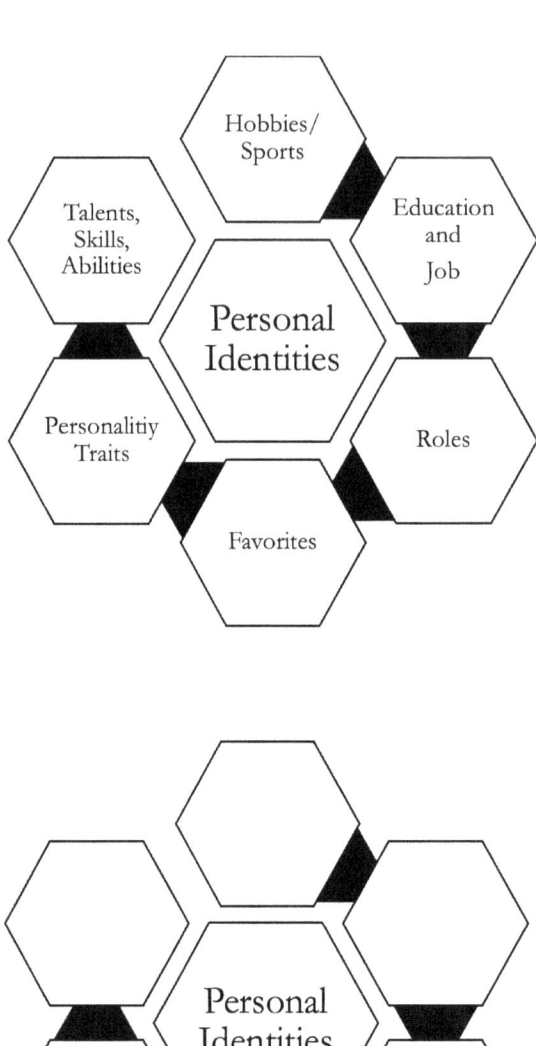

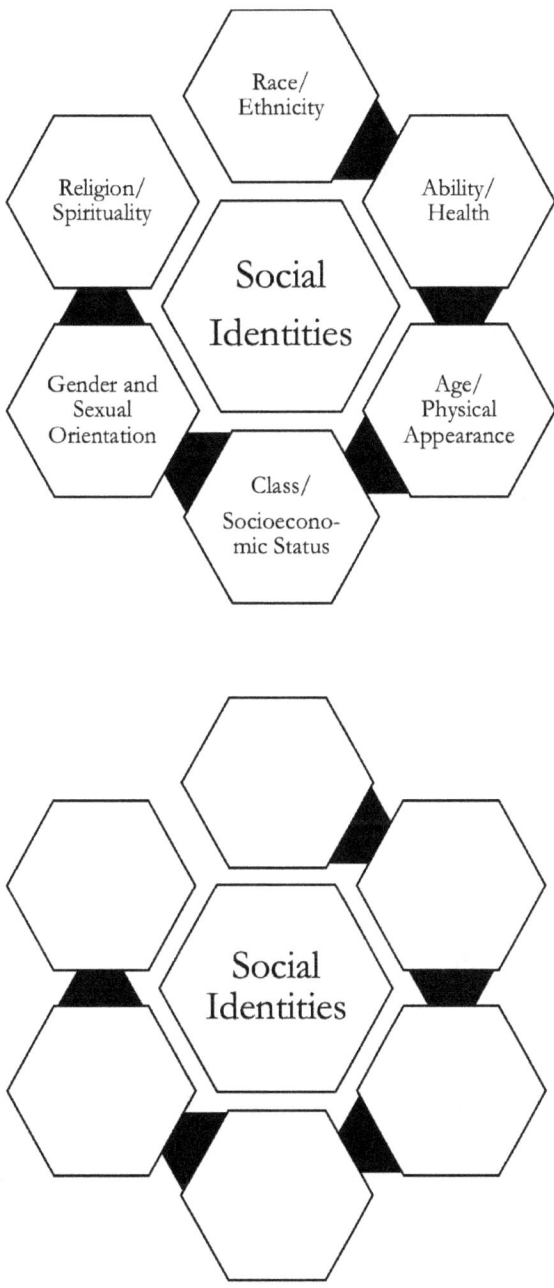

Now that you have taken some time to identify your personal and social identities, it can be helpful to reflect on how these identities impact your body image and vice versa. Consider the following questions:

> Which aspects of identity have the strongest effect on how you perceive yourself?
>
> Which have the strongest effect on how others perceive you?
>
> Are there aspects of your identity that you feel most strongly impact your body image?
>
> Are there aspects that you feel are impacted by your body image?
>
> What aspects of your privileged identities might help you improve your body image?
>
> What aspects of your marginalized identities might make it more challenging to improve your body image?
>
> Are there aspects of your identity that you feel disconnected from? How might connecting to those aspects improve your body image?
>
> What aspects of identity impact your sexuality and your sexual experiences?

Activism as Healing

Another way to work on healing the damage the outside voice did to us is to find ways to fight against that voice. This can be done through various types of activism. What comes to mind when you hear the word "activism"? Do you think of protests and marches and other grand-scale activist behavior? That is certainly one way in which we can fight the voice, but there are also some smaller everyday actions that can be considered activism.

One is making more conscious decisions regarding your spending on beauty products. Many purchases of beauty products contribute to ongoing societal body standards and reinforce the negative thought that something is wrong with us that we are trying to correct by purchasing the product. Essentially, we must consider if we are making decisions and purchases based on what we truly want or because we are told that this is what we need to do to meet beauty standards. It doesn't mean that you can't ever purchase lipstick or skin care items again. It just means you will be mindful about the purchase through the use of consciousness-raising questions. The questions are:

Why do I want this product?

Who benefits from me wanting or purchasing the item?

Does this purchase align with my values?

Here is an example.

While in the drug store picking up a prescription, I saw a display for new summer nail polish colors. Before deciding to make the purchase, I asked myself the above questions, and these were my answers:

I want the product because I enjoy painting my nails as it is a relaxing, mindful activity, and I like the way my nails look when they are painted in fun colors.

The company obviously benefits, but so do I.

There is nothing about the nail polish that goes against my values – the company does not test on animals, and I have the money to purchase it without causing any significant financial stress.

In this example, I felt good about my decision to buy the nail polish because it wasn't being influenced by beauty culture.

Here is an example of how this could look differently.

I was scrolling through social media after a long day at work. I was kind of tired and finding myself making comparisons to the smaller bodies that I was seeing, which made me feel not so great about my own body. An ad popped up for a new weight loss medication that I hadn't tried before. Without even thinking about it, I clicked the ad, but before making the purchase, I remembered to ask myself the questions. These were my answers:

I want the product because I am unhappy in my body at this moment, and I'm also tired and feeling susceptible due to engaging in comparison behaviors. I'm believing the ad's claims that I can lose weight and keep it off.

The company benefits, but I'm not so sure I will because nothing has ever worked before at keeping weight off.

Making this purchase does not align with my values as I don't believe in using medications for weight loss, I dislike pop-up ads, and I don't like the bold claims the company is making.

In this example, I felt good about deciding not to buy the product and worked on using some other coping skills to help me feel better about my body in the moment.

Another way in which you can use activism as a coping skill is by letter writing. Consider sending a letter, direct message, or email to ask for change from companies in how they advertise or to thank companies you feel are doing a great job in their representation of different bodies. Giving compliments might feel like a strange form of activism, but giving non-body or appearance-related compliments puts positive vibes out into the world and challenges the traditional way of giving compliments. By complimenting someone on something other than their appearance, you are sending the message that they are worthy beyond the way that they look. A form of giving a compliment could be by reaching out to an influencer you find inspiring and telling them how they have helped you. You could also paint rocks with inspirational messages and leave them around your neighborhood. Finally, become a model to those around you. By working on your body image issues through reading books like this or talking to a therapist, you are changing the big picture by starting with you first. Imagine what the world would look like if we all made just a few small changes.

Summing it Up

Being authentic, genuine, and wholly oneself is a key component of great sex.

In order to be fully authentic, we must be able to differentiate between our own internal thoughts and the thoughts that come from outside sources.

Understanding and identifying the origins of our thoughts and beliefs related to body image and sex is one way to start separating our authentic inside voice from the outside voice.

Challenging distressing thoughts about body image is one way to change the impact that they have on our emotions and behaviors related to sex.

Being wholly ourselves requires us to understand all the parts of our identity.

There are several ways that activism can be used to tune into our authentic selves and challenge the outside voice.

CHAPTER SIX

Transcendence and Personal Transformation - Rising Above

In the last chapter, we focused on authenticity and how being wholly ourselves allows for greater sexual satisfaction. We worked on identifying core beliefs related to body image and sexual satisfaction and learned how to start challenging them. We also covered identity and how it is essential to understand all the different parts of us in order to be completely authentic. Now, we will move towards transcendence, or rising above, by using what we have learned to further shed those core beliefs and set newer, healthier expectations of ourselves. Since we focused mostly on thoughts in Chapter Five, now we are going to look more closely at our behaviors. We will consider what our behaviors, specifically our sexual behaviors, might look like if we were able to let go of the old messaging from society, family, and friends and let in some new messaging. Through this, we will create a new cycle of thoughts and behaviors.

What is Transcendence Anyway?

In the Kleinplatz study, individuals who reported experiencing great sex had to let go, deconstruct, or overcome the restrictive ideas about sex and themselves that had become embedded in their minds. In other words, they needed to wipe the slate clean for optimal sexual experiences to be possible. For them, this was transcendence. However, this process is not easy. It will most likely involve unlearning almost everything you have learned about body image, sex, and sexuality. We will need to consider how beliefs about our bodies currently contribute to our sexual satisfaction- what do we do and what do we avoid before, during, and after sex because of our body image – and we will need to imagine what sex could look like with a different, transcendent body image. Don't worry - there is more to come on all of this.

According to Abraham Maslow,[19] self-transcendence allows us the opportunities for peak experiences in which we can transcend our own personal concerns and see from a higher perspective. Maslow believed that these peak experiences often result in strong positive emotions such as joy and peace. This sounds a lot like what the Kleinplatz participants reported. I am curious about how you are feeling reading these descriptions of transcendence. Does it feel like something that is attainable for you? It may not, and that is ok. In fact, it's very reasonable for it to feel overwhelming as it is the peak of Maslow's famous hierarchy of needs, as shown here[20].

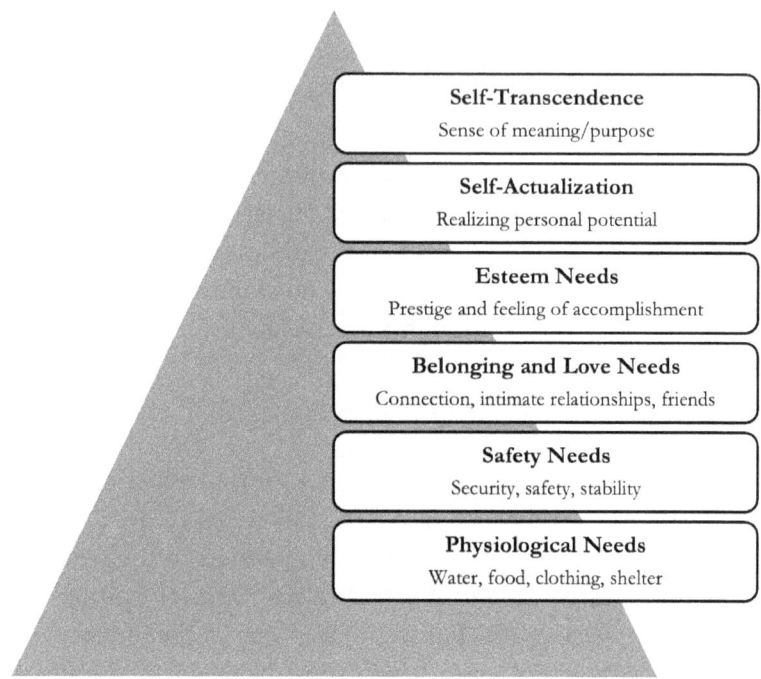

In Maslow's hierarchy, transcendence is at the top tip of the pyramid. This means that, according to Maslow, it is not achievable until the other sections of the pyramid have been fulfilled. While I do believe there is something to be said for this belief, for example, it is incredibly hard for anyone to focus on intimacy or self-esteem if they don't have food or water, I don't know that our needs always follow such a strict hierarchy. Rather, I believe needs are more fluid and that, in fact, they are more bidirectional than one-directional. For example, a sense of love and belonging can certainly make it easier to attain self-actualization, but self-actualization can also motivate us to pursue things that are important to us, like friendships, intimacy, and freedom. I also do not believe that any of the levels remain fixed once we attain them. Even things like food, clothing, shelter, and sleep can be lost to someone who has achieved esteem and self-actualization, but losing those things doesn't mean that the individual must also lose esteem and self-actualization. For these reasons, I believe that even those of us who might not have every level of the pyramid fully satisfied can still achieve moments of transcendence.

If this is true, what might transcendence look like away from Maslow's theory and in a more real-life situation? I like the measures used in Pamela Reed's Self-Transcendence Scale[21] as a guide and have included a link to the scale in Appendix D so that you can see where you fall in terms of self-transcendence. Measures on the scale include things like having hobbies or interests, being involved with other people or community when possible, helping others, having an ongoing interest in learning, and most importantly, for the purposes of this book – being able to move beyond some things that once seemed so important.

Your Best Sexual Self

It's probably no surprise to you that women who were identified as having a positive body image reported more frequent sexual encounters, more frequent orgasms, greater willingness to initiate sex and try new sexual activities, more comfort while undressing in front of their partner(s), less need to have sex with the lights off, and higher confidence in their ability to give their partner(s) pleasure than their counterparts with a negative body image [22]. These are things I am going to collectively call your best sexual self. For a moment, I would like you to consider what your best sexual self would look like. Pull out paper or a journal and think about:

> What behaviors am I engaging in now that negatively impact my sex life because of my body image?

> What would my sexual behavior look like if my body image was not a factor?

If I wasn't busy engaging in behaviors to hide my body, what could I focus on instead?

When in the past have I said no to something sexually because of my body image?

When in the past did I say yes to something sexually despite my body image and was glad I did?

What would my ultimate sexual experience look and feel like if I did not worry about body image issues?

These behaviors might feel out of reach, but let's explore some alternative messages and then revisit them to see how the new messaging might help you achieve your best sexual self.

New Messaging

One of the things that we need to do in order to move beyond, rise up, and transcend is to introduce new messaging. So far in the book, we have focused on old messaging – things we have heard, seen, or learned from places like media, friends, and family – that influenced our thoughts, feelings, and behaviors around body image and sex. Now, we are going to bring in some new messages and start to really consider how our sex lives could look different if these were the messages we focused on instead of the old ones. This will allow us to create new narratives and behaviors around our body image and our sexual satisfaction.

Body Positivity, Body Neutrality, and Body Liberation

Very likely, you have heard one or more of these terms in the last few years. They are often used interchangeably, and while they all share the commonality of helping us move towards creating a new narrative around our bodies that will, in turn, help us improve sexual satisfaction, they are each quite different. Despite their differences, I believe each one is worthy of exploration and understanding so that you can take from them what works and use that to shape your journey toward transcendence.

Body positivity is perhaps the most mainstream of these terms. It seems to be everywhere and even has its own hashtag. Body positivity urges people to love their bodies regardless of size, shape, or weight. People who promote body positivity deliver a message that tells us all bodies are worthy of respect and love. Sounds great, right? Well, it can be. I believe that body positivity is an amazing concept and is a great way to start thinking differently about our bodies and bringing in that new narrative. But nothing is perfect, and when it comes to body positivity, I believe that it's just a little too simplistic of a concept. As we know and have discussed, this is hard work! It isn't just as easy as putting on a bikini and loving your body as it is.

Body positivity also fails to recognize the privilege that some of us have that makes it easier to love our bodies. Those intersections of identity referenced earlier in the book – race, sexual orientation, age, ability, and others – complicate body positivity and make it challenging or even impossible for some individuals to achieve. This does not mean that body positivity is worthless or that it can't be helpful. Yes, yes, yes - let's be more positive and loving towards our bodies! However, let's also be aware of the limitations and challenges of body positivity and realize that the path to loving our bodies requires working to love all bodies.

Body neutrality focuses more on acceptance versus love. When looking at our bodies through a body neutrality lens, we don't need to love our bodies, but we are making a conscious choice not to look at them with hate and shame. Body neutrality recognizes that there will be times when we don't feel good about our bodies, and instead of urging the body positivity approach of utilizing positive affirmations that may at times feel inauthentic, it allows for a more impartial space out of which we can find acceptance. If this sounds familiar, it's because the thought challenging that we worked on in Chapter Five centered around body neutrality. The example I gave in that chapter was centered on moving away from the thought "My stomach is disgusting" to "This is how I look and feel today," which brings a more neutral emotional response.

Again, like body positivity, body neutrality is not without its own challenges. As it is hard to be positive, it can also be hard to be neutral when we are faced with the daily messaging coming from media, family, and friends that is so strongly skewed towards the negative. Additionally, body neutrality advocates often encourage women to focus on what their bodies can do instead of what they look like. This is great for some women – especially if we are working on improving sexual satisfaction. Think about how lovely it would be to focus solely on the pleasure our bodies can offer instead of what our bodies look like. But this type of thinking has serious limits for other women. It can be especially challenging for women who feel like their bodies have betrayed them – for example, women with disabilities or chronic illness and survivors of sexual assault. That feeling of betrayal or knowledge that there are limitations on what their bodies can do both physically and sexually can make neutrality difficult to achieve.

Where body positivity and neutrality fall short, body liberation steps in as an alternative. One of the definitions of liberation is freedom from limits on thought or behavior. Another is the act of setting someone free from imprisonment, slavery, or oppression: release. If we look at these definitions through a body image lens, we can best understand what body liberation is. It is about freedom from the limits that our thoughts about our bodies put upon our behaviors. It is about being free from the oppression that comes with being in a body that is discriminated against, whether that body is black, brown, trans, disabled, aged, or fat. Body liberation requires us to do a lot of the work we have already done in this book. For example, learning about and identifying the systems that contribute to our body image issues like we did in Chapter Five, and cultivating forgiveness and empathy like we did in Chapter Three. Body liberation brings an awareness that we are so much more than our bodies and frees us from the unrealistic expectation that bodies can't be imperfect. It normalizes imperfections and flaws as part of the human experience of owning a body and realizes that we aren't our bodies, but rather, we have bodies.

Health at Every Size

Health at Every Size (HAES) is a movement that has gained attention over the last ten years or so. HAES challenges assumptions that health is directly correlated to weight and body size and points out the damage that comes from living in a diet culture. Through the messaging, most of us have come to believe that being fat is bad and that permanent weight loss is attainable through diet changes and exercise. The reality is that being fat is not "bad" or a determinant of health, and diets often have a rebound effect in which individuals gain back the weight they lose plus some. Rather than focusing on diet and exercise as a means to lose weight and hit a certain weight or clothing size, HAES promotes flexible, intuitive eating based on hunger, nutritional needs, and pleasure while also supporting physical activities that people enjoy and encouraging participation in those activities only to the extent they choose.

This is all helpful from a body image perspective as it shifts our focus from changing our bodies to accepting them – similarly to body neutrality. It inspires body diversity, and because it is intuitive in nature, it encourages bodily introspection. But HAES isn't perfect, either. Some critics say it goes too far in disallowing or even shaming any instance of intentional weight loss, creating closed-mindedness. Regardless of its issues, HAES is helpful in our framework as we work towards integrating alternative messaging into our lives because it allows an alternative to diet culture and encourages us to create more balanced and realistic expectations of health, body size, and weight. That, in my opinion, is a step in the right direction.

Now that you have learned the difference between body positivity, body neutrality, and body liberation and know what HAES is, let's take some time to reflect.

Where do you think you are in your journey – body positivity, neutrality, or liberation? Can you be in more than one of these spaces?

What will help you move forward to the ultimate space of body liberation? If you feel you are already there, what can help keep you there?

What expectations do you currently have about bodies? How do these expectations impact your sexuality and sexual satisfaction?

How would HAES help you with moving forward toward body liberation?

What are some more realistic expectations you can start to have about your body? How might these expectations change the way you approach sex?

Good Enough Sex

Most of the messaging from the world we live in tells us that sexual satisfaction or pleasure comes exclusively from orgasms. The problem with this limited view is that it does not encompass the multitude of ways in which humans can experience sexual and sensual pleasure. Further problematic, this view frames sexual encounters in a performance-based way – sex becomes a pass/fail activity. If you can't have an orgasm, then you are failing at sex. When linked with body image, it can be perceived as yet another failure. Not only are we failing to meet the idealized body standard, but we are also failing at being sexually satisfied at the same time.

The good news is that the messaging we've received is wrong. Sex does not have to be performative in order to be satisfying. This view started shifting in the sex therapy world around 2007 when the focus in treatment went from arousal and orgasm to desire, pleasure, and satisfaction. The Good Enough Sex Model (GES)[23] is centered around acceptance and realistic expectations, particularly involving female orgasms. GES recognizes that female orgasms are wildly unique and occur in a multitude of ways – none of which are right or wrong. GES also emphasizes that sex is more than just biological functioning and encourages us to redefine sex in a way that is meaningful for us personally. Sex does not have to be intercourse. It can be cuddling, touching, erotic play, or anything that brings pleasure. Under the GES model, sex involves feelings and meaning and views them as important as physicality. Sexual satisfaction involves feeling good about yourself as a sexual woman, with desire and satisfaction as more important than arousal and orgasm.

GES also acknowledges the role that satisfaction has on our sexual self-esteem. When we feel sexually satisfied, we feel better about ourselves sexually. I would even take that a step further; when we feel good about ourselves sexually, it can trickle into our general sense of self, raising our overall self-esteem, which includes our body image. When our body image improves, our sexual satisfaction also improves, and the cycle continues. I visualize it like this:

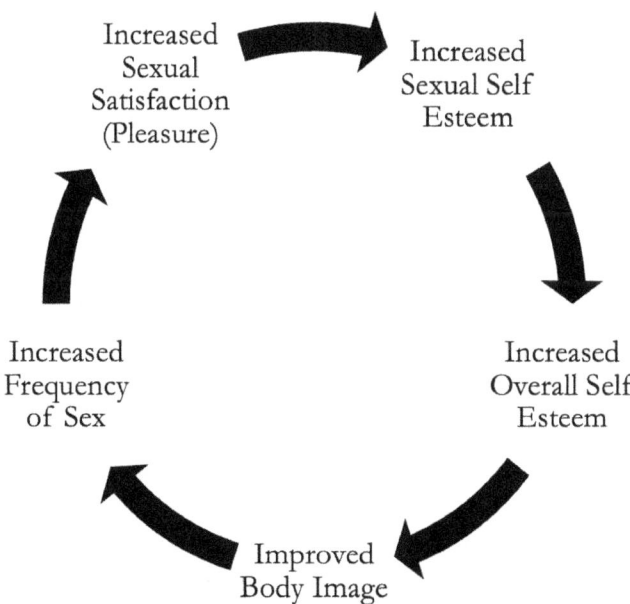

Conversely, irrational thinking subverts sexual self-esteem, our overall sense of self, and body image, which can lower our interest in sex. If irrational thinking about sex and our bodies gets inserted anywhere into this cycle, it will throw things off and cause issues. Before we go further, let's take an opportunity to pause and consider the following:

> Using GES as a guide, how would you redefine sex for yourself?
>
> What kinds of irrational thoughts or misinformation do you think get in the way of the healthy sex cycle described above?
>
> What could change for you sexually if you were able to accept GES instead of striving for something that may not be realistic?
>
> How do body image issues get in the way of GES?

Desire and Context

In addition to the message that orgasm equals sexual satisfaction, which GES works to challenge, popular culture also tells us that optimum sexual satisfaction is spontaneous and frequent. Think of all those scenes in the movies where two people lock eyes across the room, and within five minutes, they are engaged in hot and heavy sex, which typically consists of a penis inserted into a vagina. This messaging can result in unrealistic expectations of self and partner(s) and can perpetuate anxiety, shame, and guilt for people who do not experience sex in this specifically defined way, particularly trans or queer women or women with certain disabilities.

Spontaneous desire, or what is described above and seen in most media depictions of sex, is possible and does happen for some women. But this number is low, with only about 15 percent[24] of female-identifying individuals reporting this type of desire. More typically occurring is something called responsive desire. Responsive desire is driven by a variety of factors, including touch, physical closeness, and feelings of affection. This type of desire requires creating time and space for intimacy rather than just expecting it to happen out of nowhere. This can be particularly challenging for individuals in long-term relationships as desire does tend to be more spontaneous at the beginning of a relationship. Holding on to the expectation that sex and desire should continue to be spontaneous can be unrealistic and is something that needs to be challenged for transcendence to occur.

It is important for me to note that even if you fall into the category of having more of a spontaneous desire pattern, there are things that can shut off that desire – such as a negative body image. This is an example of a contextual factor that has a huge impact on desire. Contextual factors, by their definition, are fluid. The way I feel about my body on one day can lead to a different type of desire than it might on a different day when I'm feeling more or less positive about it. Knowing that contextual factors exist and aren't set in stone can help us with transcending the idea or message that something is wrong with us for not wanting sex at certain times because of certain factors going on in our lives or our brains. Consider this as another opportunity for reflection:

Which desire style do I most often relate to?

How often does my body image impact the context around my desire?

By having a more realistic expectation of my desired style, can I challenge old beliefs and make changes to my behavior?

Using Your New Messaging to Create Change

After reading and learning about these alternative messages about body image and sex, let's take a look at how we can use them to move towards that best sexual self that we talked about earlier in the chapter. First, let's reflect one more time on how this information can help to reach transcendence:

Have I been looking at sex through a performative lens?

How have my body image issues and lack of understanding of body liberation and HAES impacted my idea of a "stellar sexual performance"?

How can focusing on pleasure versus performance help me to improve my sexual experiences?

How might sexual pleasure help me feel better about my body and lead to body liberation?

What is a more realistic and reasonable behavioral expectation that I can have of myself and my body during a sexual encounter?

Now, let's examine your current sexual behaviors that are influenced by your body image. Go back to the questions you answered earlier in this chapter about your best sexual self and choose a behavior that you would like to change. In this example, I am going to focus on the behavior of turning the lights off during sex.

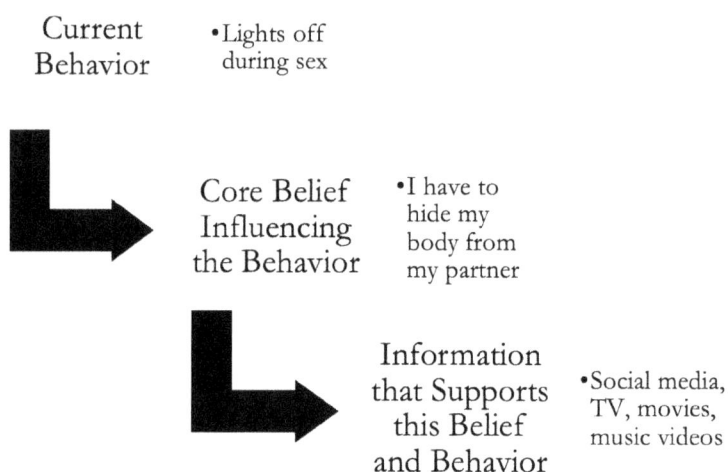

Let's now consider the new messaging and information that we've learned. Can any of it be applied as information that does not support this core belief and behavior or challenges it in any way? List that information here or in your journal:

_____

_____

_____

_____

Taking the new information that you have listed above, let's now revisit the behavior diagram. Instead of turning the lights off, the desired behavior that will lead to my best sexual self is keeping the lights on.

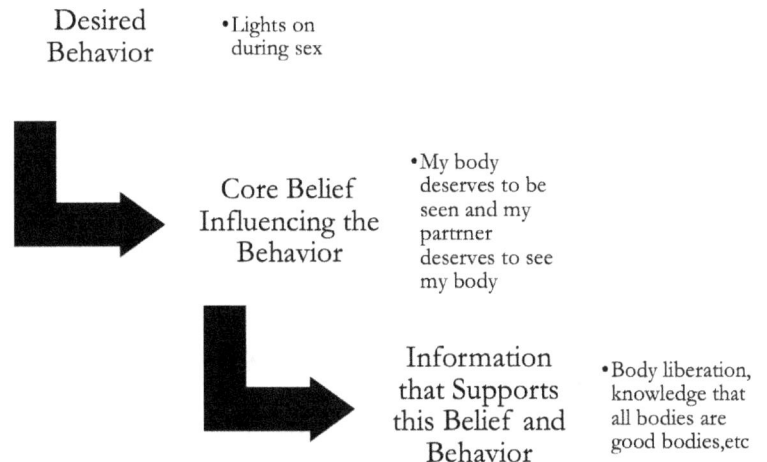

Here is a blank version that you can use to work through how the new information you have learned can help support the behaviors that will foster transcendence and lead to being your best sexual self.

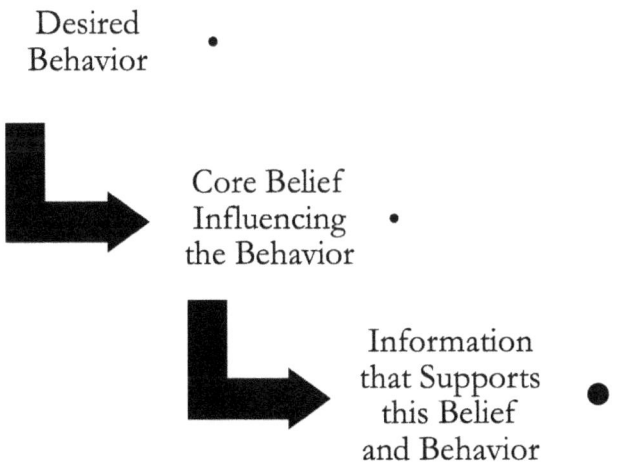

Summing it Up

Transcendence, which comes from personal transformation, is another key component of great sex.

Wiping the slate clean of old faulty thinking that came from media, family, and friends to make room for new, accurate thinking is an important part of transcendence. In other words, we need to work to move beyond some things that once seemed so important to us and create new, more realistic expectations of ourselves.

Learning alternative ways to look at body image and sexual satisfaction, like body liberation, HAES, GES, and others, can help us reset our expectations around sex and bodies.

Once we can integrate these new expectations into our everyday thoughts, we can start to change our sexual behaviors and achieve transcendence.

CHAPTER SEVEN

If You Can't Have Fun, What's the Sense in Doing It?

In Chapter Six, we tackled some pretty big ideas related to body image and sex. We introduced concepts like body liberation, health at every size, and good enough sex, and we learned about different types of desire – all with the goal of transcending or rising above. In this chapter, we will hopefully have a little more fun. According to the participants in the Kleinplatz study, to have great sex, individuals need to actively seek out new sexual experiences and information and be willing to learn and explore consistently. This need for fun and exploration will drive what we discuss in this chapter.

We will focus on what feels good about sex and how to figure out what you like and don't like sexually by building a sexual template or menu. We will consider what it might be like to view physical activity in a new way. We will learn about desire and sexual satisfaction through the sexual excitation system and sexual inhibition lens, then change the context of arousal based on this information. We will consider how body image might get in the way of the willingness to try new things and how trying new things can help us feel better about our bodies. And finally, we will talk about moving our bodies in a way that focuses on fun.

Sexual Responsiveness (AKA Desire) – What's Your Sexual Temperament?

Over the years, there has been a lot of debate and evolution around different theories and models of women's desire and sexual responsiveness. In the late 1990s, Erick Janssen and John Bancroft developed what has come to be known as the dual control model. This model expands beyond prior models of human sexuality, which focused mainly on physical arousal, and considers what contributes to desire and how you respond to different sexual stimuli[25]. Emily Nagoski talks about the dual control model extensively in her book *Come As You Are*. The book is phenomenal, and I highly recommend it. Here, I will summarize it in a way that makes sense for our specific discussion about body image and sexual satisfaction.

Basically, our sexual response is made up of two systems – the sexual excitation system, or SES, and the sexual inhibition system, or SIS. The SES is referred to by Nagoski and others as the accelerator or gas pedal, while the SIS is referred to as the brakes. In other words, the SES is sensitive to our turn-ons, and the SIS is sensitive to our turn-offs. When the SIS is more focused on turn-offs than the SES is on turn-ons, we lose desire or interest in sex. Just about anything can impact both the SES and SIS. For our purposes, we need to acknowledge that body image issues are a definite brake. However, imagine for a moment that you can use what you have learned in this book to improve your body image, feel more comfortable and confident in your body, and receive appreciation from your partner(s). Now, *that* is something I believe would definitely hit the gas pedal.

While body image is the main element that we are concerned with when it comes to considering the importance of SES/SIS, it is also important to have a full understanding of your sexual temperament. There is a sexual temperament questionnaire at the end of Chapter Two in *Come as You Are,* and I have also included a link to an electronic version of it in Appendix D. I encourage you to check this out as it can help to normalize your overall experience of sexual arousal and desire.

I'd like to acknowledge that desire and pleasure can be confusing for many women, particularly survivors of sexual trauma. If this is true for you, I highly recommend the book *Reclaiming Pleasure: A Sex-Positive Guide for Moving Past Sexual Trauma & Living a Passionate Life* by Holly Richmond, Ph.D. The nature of sexual trauma itself can make you feel like you are not worthy of pleasure and can make it hard to trust your body to identify what is truly pleasurable and what is not. This is partially due to something called arousal non-concordance, which can be helpful for everyone to understand regardless of whether you have experienced sexual assault or not. Nagoski has a lot to say about this in *Come as You Are* but sums it up by stating, "Sexual arousal may or may not have anything to do with what is happening in your genitals."[26] In other words, just because something feels good physically does not mean you like it, and just because you don't have an immediate genital response doesn't mean you don't like it. Keeping this in mind while you explore what might be on and off your menu is important. As you think about the things that might bring you pleasure physically and cause desire, consider also any emotional response or "gut response" that you experience.

What's On (And Off) Your Sexual Menu?

Now that we understand desire, turn-ons, and turn-offs, let's get into exploring what interests you have sexually. There are a few different things that we will consider, the first being your sexual template or menu. How is our sexual template or menu created? Partly through messaging that we receive from society, family, and friends. Here is an example. Maybe you were told by a family member or got the message from your religion, TV, or movies that "nice girls" don't do anything other than vanilla sex (conventional, stereotypical sex). Or maybe you received a message that only sluts or "nasty girls" have fantasies, are into kink, or want and like anything other than missionary style. Maybe you had a partner who yucked your yum by telling you that what you wanted to try was gross. Or maybe you found the first thing you tried sexually to be "good enough" and never felt too compelled to try anything else. If you like a little more spice or just want to try new things in the bedroom, these kinds of messages can be problematic and confusing. They can cause shame and result in us not exploring what feels good, what we find sexy, and what we desire.

The way that we feel about our bodies also contributes to our willingness to explore our sexual menus. If we have a negative body image, we probably aren't going to be open to using our bodies to explore our sexuality. But even worse, we might learn through the messaging from society, family, and friends that our sexual body parts – and the fluids, sounds, smells, and tastes that come along with those body parts - are something to feel shame and disgust around we can further shut down any sexual exploration. For example, I once worked with a client who grew up believing that vaginas smelled and tasted "fishy." Because of this, she was hesitant to let any partner get too close to her vagina. Oral sex was off the table for a long time, despite a curiosity and interest in it. It took some time, but she was eventually able to use learning and challenge her beliefs enough to allow a partner to perform oral sex. Which, by the way, she ended up loving. Let's take a moment to consider the following:

What early messages did I get about sex and bodies?

How did these messages impact my willingness to explore and try new things in the bedroom?

What else gets in the way of truly exploring my sexual likes?

How do I think expanding my ideas of sexual pleasure and fun could help my body image and vice versa?

Now, we will work on creating your sexual menu. I like to break down the sexual menu into a few different categories – appetizers or foreplay, main course or whatever you consider the most important and most fulfilling aspect of sex, dessert or what happens after the main course, and the side dishes which can include kinks, fantasies, and fetishes. Remember, when building your menu, we are considering not only current and known likes but also things you would like to explore and are willing to try.

Let's start with appetizers. When you think of foreplay, what does that include? Consider when the sexual encounter starts for you. Is it when you are physically with your partner(s), or is it earlier than that? Does it start with a thought? A sexy text message or suggestion to your partner(s) for what you'd like to do later? What are you or your partner(s) wearing? Does it include setting the scene with candlelight or leading into things with a romantic dinner? Would cuddling or sensual massage be part of the appetizer section?

Onto the main course. This does not have to include intercourse or penetration and may or may not result in orgasms for you or your partner(s). Think about what you consider to be the most important aspect of your sexual encounters. What brings you the most pleasure? What is the most fulfilling? What body parts are included? Does it include sex toys? What about the length of the encounter?

Are quickies a part of your main course menu? Where is the sex happening – indoors, outdoors, shower, bed, somewhere else?

Now for some dessert. What do you want or need after the main course is finished? Just because the main course is over doesn't mean there has to be an abrupt stop to sex. Is this when cuddling is important? Do you want to take a selfie with or without your partner(s)? For real - it's a thing! Is this a time when you'd like to debrief – which is essential after an encounter involving BDSM (bondage and discipline, dominance and submission) - but can also be helpful for any sexual encounter? This is when you can talk to your partner(s) about what you and they liked and didn't like. You will also want to consider things like if you are okay with you and/or your partner(s) going to sleep right after the main course. What about a shower either solo or with your partner(s)? Include anything that might be important to you after the main course is over.

And finally, the side dishes. These are the extras that we can sprinkle in with the main course or with the appetizers, including kinks, fantasies, and fetishes. This is where you consider things like elements of BDSM, including restraints, impact play, or power play, or consider anything kinky or different, such as sensation play using things like feathers, ice cubes, or hot wax. Fantasies also fall under the side dish category – some of the more common fantasies are multiple partner sex, role-playing, or gender-bending sexual expressions, like cross-dressing or pegging[27]. Even trying something new, like a new position, can fall into the fantasy and side dish category. The sky really is the limit when it comes to side dishes.

Because side dishes can be limitless, they are often the most difficult part of creating the sexual menu. To really explore the side dishes, you will need to lean in and open up your erotic imagination. One way to do this is to use your body to explore pleasure through your senses. Below, you will find each sense listed with several examples of what could be considered pleasurable or sexy, along with a space to fill in what is sexy to you. While reading the examples, consider what brings you pleasure, how you know, and what pleasure feels like for you:

Sight

- Stilettos, lingerie, business suit, ripped jeans, facial hair, freckles, dancers, curvy bodies, mountains, ocean, fireplace, bubble bath, tattoos, myself in lingerie, people kissing on the beach, people having sex (movies, pornography or live)

  When I use my sense of sight, I find _____ sexy.

Smell

- Vanilla, pumpkin, apples, pine, leather, the woods, bubblegum, pie, cookies, smoke, perfume, cologne, soap, rain, flowers, my partner after a shower, candles burning, crisp air, incense, roses, body odor, muskiness

  When I use my sense of smell, I find _____ sexy.

Touch

- Silk or satin, lace, leather, hair, skin, pressure, feathers, grass, paintbrush, water, ice, sand in my toes, laying outside naked, being spanked or spanking, tight jeans, not wearing underwear

  When I use my sense of touch, I find _____ sexy.

Hear

- A deep or soft voice, singing, music, drums, waves crashing, rain, laughter, glasses clinking, engine revving, being complimented, kissing sounds, sex sounds, dirty talk, the buzz of a sex toy

  When I use my sense of hearing, I find _____ sexy.

Taste

- Red meat, cake, avocado, wine, champagne, mint, cinnamon gum, berries, ice-cream, oysters, chocolate, feeding my partner or being fed, my partners lips, skin, or other body parts

  When I use my sense of taste, I find _____ sexy

Using porn can also be a good way to get your sexual imagination going. I get it. Porn is not for everyone. It has a lot of disadvantages, including that it contributes significantly to the media messaging around what women's bodies are supposed to look like, how we are supposed to perform, and what sex is supposed to be like. But before you decide completely if porn is for you or not, consider that an advantage of porn is that it can provide a greater sexual self-awareness that could be helpful in expanding your sexual menu. If you decide to use porn either on your sexual menu or in creating your sexual menu, please be mindful of the porn you are consuming. There has been a movement in recent years toward creating more ethical porn. Ethical porn is porn that is consensual, does not involve trafficking, underaged individuals, or coercion, shows both fantasy and real-world situations, and is inclusive of a diverse range of bodies. When viewing porn, pay attention to not only how you are responding physically but how you are responding emotionally, and do not engage with porn that leaves you feeling shameful, guilty, or any emotion that doesn't feel good.

If this is all overwhelming, it's okay. No one has an exhaustive list in their heads of every sexual possibility. Use the questions here as a guide, and check out some of the resources in Appendix D to help you. There are links to different "yes/no/maybe" checklists that each have a variety of sexual activities that you can complete alone or with your partner(s). If having conversations about your sexual menu feels scary, there is also an app called Spicer, where you and your partner(s) download and answer questions privately about what you might find interesting, and then the app syncs your answers, providing any matches. This is a great way to get the topic flowing while minimizing vulnerability.

Now, let's take all of this and put it together to create your sexual menu. I have provided an example as well as space for you to enter your own yes, no, and maybe responses. I recognize that the space here is small, so please feel free to use your journal or another method that feels comfortable to create your menu if you would like. Some people even use Excel spreadsheets to do this exercise! It can also be helpful to consider stepping outside of using yes/maybe/no as your options by creating a rating scale that you use to define your interest in something. For example, a scale might go from zero to five with the following descriptors – 0= hard limit no, 1 = soft limit maybe, 2=I'll try it at least once, 3 = I could take it or leave it, 4 = I'm interested, and 5 = definitely yes.

Sample Sexual Menu

Appetizers	Main Course	Side Dishes	Dessert
Yes	**Yes**	**Yes**	**Yes**
• Sexting- dirty talk only -throughout the day • Full body massage • Candlelight dinner • Making out	• In bed • Using toys • Penetration	• Light bondage • Feeding berries and whipped cream to partner	• Cuddling • Bubble bath together
	Maybe		**Maybe**
	• Outdoors • Mutual masurbation	• Watching ethical porn together	• Debriefing • Take a selfie
Maybe			**No**
• Sexting nudes • Washing each other in the shower • Wearing lingerie	**No**	**Maybe**	• Sleep • Talk about things other than sex
	• Anal penetration	• Light impact play -spanking • Hot wax	
		No	
		• Nipple clamps • Feathers (allergic)	
No			
• PDA • Foot massages (ticklish)			

Appetizers	Main Course	Side Dishes	Dessert
Yes	Yes	Yes	Yes
Maybe	Maybe	Maybe	Maybe
No	No	No	No

Now that you have taken some time to create your sexual menu consider the following:

How do my body image issues contribute to me not experiencing more with the things on my sexual menu?

What tools from the book so far can help make this easier?

How might engaging in more sexual fun and exploration help my body image?

Move Your Body

Most of us avoid exercise or view it as a chore due to the attachment we have created about it being one of the main ways to achieve the perfect body. Much of our purposeful movement occurs due to a sense of obligation or to avoid shame and guilt. But moving our bodies can be fun! In fact, exercise for enjoyment may be associated with positive body image. In a 2010 study, adolescents with high levels of body satisfaction reported viewing exercise as a natural, important, and joyful part of life[28]. These adolescents explained that while they appreciated the health benefits, they also viewed exercise as more than just a way to lose weight or control the size or shape of the body. The message that we can take from this is simple. If we can look at movement and exercise as something fun and a way to honor our bodies, it can help attune to our bodies in ways that will reduce negative body image. Taking this information into consideration, let's take a moment to reflect on the following:

> What types of body movement (exercise or physical activity) have you done that you did not enjoy? Why do you think you engaged in this type of body movement? How did doing that make you feel emotionally? Physically?

> When was the last time you engaged in body movement you enjoyed? How was that experience different from the experiences you didn't enjoy?

> What are the body movement activities that you used to or still enjoy? How often do you participate in these activities? If you don't participate in them, why not?

> What do you think might happen to your overall body image if you were to focus on integrating the body movement activities you enjoy the most into your life on a more regular basis?

> What might change for you sexually if you started to move your body in a fun-centric way more often?

> If a body movement activity you previously enjoyed is not currently attainable for whatever reason, are there options for adaptations or similar replacement activities?

Some of the above questions assumed that you already know what body movement activities you enjoy. But what if you don't? That's okay. You might not know right away what feels good because you've only ever focused on what doesn't. Lucky for you, I have included a website in Appendix D where you can find a long list of physical activities. The list includes some of the more typical things like going for a walk or playing a sport, as well as some not-so-obvious things like having a dance party around the house, flying a kite, and playing frisbee.

I want to acknowledge that for various reasons, body movement may not be easy or possible for everyone. In the absence of being able to move your whole body, let's also consider the alternative of doing something that uses parts of your body to bring pleasure or enjoyment in other ways. Maybe that is setting aside a few minutes to just give yourself a hand massage. Maybe it is putting on your softest, fuzziest pair of socks to wear around the house. Maybe it's doing a refreshing face mask or putting on a full face of makeup for no reason other than it makes you feel good.

While moving our bodies outside the bedroom might not immediately correlate with better sex, it can help with overall body image and better body attunement, both of which can lead to more enjoyable sex. It also contributes to overall pleasure by training your brain to associate your body with pleasure and enjoyment instead of shame and negative experiences.

Summing it Up

Fun and exploration are another component of great sex.

Understanding desire and arousal is important before exploring new sexual interests in order to minimize shame and self-judgment.

Our body image can impact our willingness to explore and expand our sexual menus.

Sexual menus consist of appetizers or foreplay, a main course or whatever you consider the most important and most fulfilling aspect of sex, dessert or what happens after the main course, and the side dishes, which can include kinks, fantasies, and fetishes.

Creating a sexual menu involves exploring each aspect of sex, exploring what we are interested in, and what gives pleasure.

We can use our five senses to explore what brings pleasure.

Reframing how we look at exercises and body movement can be another way to have fun and feel better about our bodies, leading to better sex.

CHAPTER EIGHT

Vulnerability - Letting Yourself Be Seen

In Chapter Seven, we focused on sex that is explorative and fun. We learned about arousal and desire and then worked on creating a sexual menu or template. We also considered how shifting our mindset around body movement away from a place of punishment and duty to a place of fun can help body image and make sex more fun, too. Creating the sexual menu required a willingness to open yourself to new ideas and sexual possibilities, which took a certain amount of risk and might have felt scary. In other words, it required you to be vulnerable. Vulnerability requires being ready, willing, and able to learn from opportunities when they appear, which in turn requires courage, fearlessness, mental flexibility, and the ability to stay grounded. The openness to trying new things doesn't just include the new items on your sexual menu but is essential in using all of the new skills and ideas you've learned so far in the book.

Vulnerability contributes to great sex because it creates a space where you can say and do anything and still feel desired and experience pleasure. But getting to that space isn't easy. Just seeing the word vulnerability might invoke a certain amount of fear and anxiety-most of us do not like being vulnerable. The good news is that if you have read the other chapters in this book, you have already learned a lot about what it takes to be vulnerable. An awareness of thoughts and emotions from Chapters One and Five, using your moral compass or the values you identified in Chapter Two, expressing yourself honestly and setting boundaries from Chapters Two and Four, and learning to appreciate your body from Chapter Three – all of these are pieces of the vulnerability puzzle. In this chapter, we will consider some other elements of vulnerability, learn how to cultivate trust (with yourself and your partner(s)), lean into fear, and claim your version of sexy.

What is Vulnerability

Merriam-Webster defines vulnerability as "1: capable of being physically or emotionally wounded; 2: open to attack or damage"[29]. I don't know about you, but that sounds pretty scary. Who wants to be wounded or damaged? In her book *Daring Greatly*, Brené Brown offers a slightly softer description of vulnerability: "uncertainty, risk, and emotional exposure[30]." While I love Brené, this still isn't something that sounds fun.

To help make vulnerability feel less scary, I often encourage clients to identify their own definitions of vulnerability and to consider what vulnerability means to them. I challenge them to stop looking at vulnerability as a bad and scary thing but rather as a good thing. As you can imagine, clients sometimes end up looking at me like I have lost my mind – vulnerability a good thing? But vulnerability is not only a good thing – it can be beautiful and even fun. It can generate creativity and joy. It can also provide a sense of belonging and connection. I don't know if we could have meaningful relationships without being vulnerable, as doing so is a great way to strengthen your bond with someone.

Here is an example of how vulnerability can nurture connection and joy and even result in fun experiences. Imagine a woman who has acquired a mobility impairment due to a car accident. She is paraplegic with no sensation or voluntary movement below the waist. In order to have a sex life with her male partner that includes penetrative sex, they must use a device in their bedroom that can lift her safely with a sling under her buttocks. There are multiple ways in which she must be vulnerable and trust him. First, she must trust that he will operate the device appropriately so she doesn't fall and become further injured. She also must trust him in applying lubricant liberally so her delicate vaginal tissues are not harmed by penetrative sex. Additionally, they might try different positions using the lifting device, which would make her more vulnerable. Through her ability to lean in and be vulnerable with her partner, they can have fun and maintain an intimate bond and even use humor as the device may make noises or swing a bit too much one way or the other.

Take a moment here to consider what vulnerability means to you, particularly in terms of your body image and sexual satisfaction:

How have you traditionally defined vulnerability? Where do you think this definition came from?

How does your definition of vulnerability hold you back from improving your body image and/or having a more satisfying sex life?

What does being vulnerable feel like for you?

What do you think you need to start being more vulnerable today?

Trust as a Path to Vulnerability

Being vulnerable doesn't require trust, but trust is something that can make vulnerability a lot easier. When we trust that the person we are being vulnerable with won't hurt us, it can be a little easier to lean in and share. Incidentally, being vulnerable also builds trust. By leaning in, sharing, and seeing that the person we are being vulnerable with won't hurt us, trust grows with that person. When it comes to vulnerability, trusting others isn't the only type of trust that is important – trusting yourself also matters here.

Self-Trust

Being able to trust yourself will increase confidence and make it easier to be vulnerable with others. Trusting yourself is a form of self-compassion. It is saying, "I know who I am and what is important to me," and using that information to facilitate your decisions. Part of self-trust includes the ability to trust your body. Negative body image can make this difficult. The mindfulness practice of body scan, outlined in Chapter One, is one thing that can help with knowing and trusting your body because it encourages tuning in and paying attention to your body's sensations and signals. Focusing on what is happening in your body will allow you to learn what your body needs and wants at any given time. This is not only an excellent way to learn to trust your body but also to have an appreciation for it and its ability to provide feedback and cues.

Another aspect of trusting your body is tuning into your gut feelings or intuition. A common barrier to this is not knowing the difference between what your gut is telling you and anxiety. Sometimes, we dismiss our instincts as anxieties that need to be challenged, or we misinterpret anxiety as a gut feeling. When we effectively utilize our intuition, we can learn to trust ourselves better. So, how exactly do you tell the difference between a gut feeling and anxiety? Here is a chart that can help you to distinguish between the two:

Anxiety		Gut Feeling/Instinct
Tend to focus on outcomes that are out of your control.		Lead us in a clear direction and is based on what we can control.
Tend to be more future based.	OR	A basic and immediate feeling – in the here and now.
Doesn't let up – remains persistent even after a decision is made.		Usually resolves a decision.
Accompanied by uncertainty.		Feels more concrete.
Does not always have a "knowable" answer.		Easily tested and verified, offering certainty, even if it is difficult to understand.

Keeping these differences in mind, consider how ignoring your instincts might be maintaining your negative body image and getting in the way of sexual pleasure. For example, a client was experiencing some strong concerns at the beginning of a relationship, but because of how she felt about her body, she was dismissing her intuition as being anxious. She told herself that she needed to stop focusing on the negative aspects of the relationship because no one else would want her anyway. She stayed in the relationship, and when she started to have sex with this partner, she experienced pain – which she had never experienced before during sex. All physical issues were ruled out, and I encouraged her to consider what her body might be telling her. For her, the pain meant that her body was screaming at her, telling her that this partner was not good for her. Because she ignored her initial gut feelings, her body persisted and found another way to send her the message. Amazingly, she was able to use this experience to not only leave the relationship but she gained a new appreciation for her body, which led to a huge improvement in her overall body image.

Focusing on your strengths can be beneficial in cultivating self-trust. The first step is identifying your strengths. This is not always easy for someone with body image issues, as sometimes the negative thoughts we have about our bodies can permeate into our overall sense of self, so instead of asking you to come up with these strengths cold, I'm providing a short list to get you started. This is not a comprehensive list of every possible strength you could possess, so please feel free to add any that you feel apply to you.

Adaptable	Affectionate	Appreciative	Brave	Cheerful
Creative	Curious	Dedicated	Efficient	Fair
Funny	Honest	Hopeful	Intelligent	Observant
Patient	Perceptive	Punctual	Resilient	Self-Aware

Now that you have identified some of your strengths, for each one, consider the following:

How can you tap into this strength to help improve your body image?

How can this strength help you be more vulnerable and possibly lead to letting go in a way that can bring greater sexual satisfaction?

Trusting Your Partner(s)

Increasing trust with your partner(s) is one way to make practicing vulnerability a bit easier. One way to do this is to share your secrets and fears with them. This can include the way we feel about our bodies and the things we desire sexually. We can also use a sense of humor to approach this sharing. By nature, sex and the things that happen during sex can be funny, absurd, and sometimes embarrassing. Bodies, especially two bodies creating friction, make funny noises, pets stare or try to get in the way, muscles cramp up, we lose balance or stamina, and many other things can be funny or awkward during sex. Make a point to talk to your partner(s) about these things and practice vulnerability by letting yourselves laugh at them.

In Chapter Four, I proposed a communication model that can make difficult conversations a little easier. You can use this model to foster trust and practice vulnerability. Some other ways that can make being vulnerable a little easier are:

Use a couple's notebook/journal

Use an app- Paired, Gottman Card Deck, and Intimately Us are all great for this

Talk about sex at nonsexual times

Set the scene for the conversation – make it a comfortable environment

Use puppets or an accent

Speak in the third person

Schedule regular times for conversations that can include talking about body image and sex – my clients sometimes call these "state of the relationship meetings" or "fireside chats"

Additionally, in order to build trust, it is important to learn listening skills as well as talking skills. Start by being present. If you are unable to be in the moment with your partner(s) when they want to share something with you, let them know you don't have capacity and ask to table the conversation until you are better able to listen. Making eye contact shows your partner(s) that you are interested and present. Being curious is another quality of good listening. You can do this by asking clarifying questions or stating, "Help me to understand better." This is more helpful than making assumptions. Reflective listening also helps because it offers an opportunity for clarification. To be a reflective listener, summarize or paraphrase what your partner(s) said, reflecting their statement back to them. Also, always thank your partner(s) for sharing.

Eye contact is a way to connect with your partner(s) and build trust because when we look into someone's eyes, we can focus on picking up their feelings as well as communicating to them ours[31]. A simple eye gazing exercise is something that can purposefully integrate eye contact into your relationship. It can feel awkward at first, but by facing that awkwardness, you are also practicing vulnerability! Here are the steps to use for eye gazing:

> **Step #1** - Sit face-to-face one to two feet away from your partner. Start by closing your eyes and taking a couple of deep breaths. As you breathe deeply, set an intention for trust by saying to yourself, "I will allow my partner to see me for where I am within in this moment."
>
> **Step #2** - Count to three with your partner, and on the count of three, slowly open your eyes and meet your partner's gaze.
>
> **Step #3** - Look into your partner's eyes for an agreed-upon amount of time. Since this can feel uncomfortable, start with 30 seconds to one minute. Focus on gazing, not staring. The difference is subtle but important. Both are intense, but staring has a more rude and aggressive feel while gazing is done with the intention of admiration and curiosity. Avoid talking. Since you aren't staring, feel free to blink as needed. If any thoughts enter your mind during the exercise, gently acknowledge them without judgment and refocus your attention to gazing at your partner.

After the exercise, take time to talk to your partner about the experience and how it felt to be vulnerable. Consider how it might feel to integrate a version of this during your sexual encounters and how the trust that potentially comes from that might lead to increased pleasure.

Fear as a Roadblock to Vulnerability

As I mentioned earlier in the chapter, by its very definition, vulnerability is scary. Additionally, shame is a breeding ground for fear. When we consider how prevalent shame is with negative body image, it is no surprise that it's incredibly difficult to be vulnerable when suffering from body image issues. The thing is, we often forget that we have a choice regarding what to do with our fears. We can nurture it and let it control our behaviors, or we can lean in and do the things we fear anyway. Way back in the introduction of this book, I wrote about the bikinis in Italy and how inspiring they were for me. Seeing bikinis on all different types of bodies made me want to lean into the fear and wear a bikini. Was wearing a bikini to the beach where other people could see me scary the first time? Yup. But I did it anyway. I choose what to do with the fear. I leaned in. And while it's not yet completely comfortable for me to wear a bikini to the beach, it's a little easier to lean into the fear each time.

One quick and easy way to help minimize the impact fear can have on our ability to be vulnerable is to ask yourself a series of questions that I like to call the power of threes:

Will the thing I'm afraid of matter in three hours?

Will the thing I'm afraid of matter in three days?

Will the thing I'm afraid of matter in three months?

Will the thing I'm afraid of matter in three years?

Let's look at this with an example. I had a client who was having trouble deciding what to wear to a baby shower. She had a dress she loved but felt a little uncomfortable in as it was short and showed some parts of her legs that she felt insecure about. Her fear was that people would judge her. We talked through the power of threes questions, and she was able to bring in logic to counterbalance her fear. She identified that the fear of judgment wasn't rational because most of the attendees would be focusing their attention on the momma-to-be. She also realized that even if someone was judging her, it would not really matter once the shower was over. This exercise helped her to lean in and be vulnerable. She wore the dress and told me in our next session that she had a great time at the shower.

Managing our expectations is another way to reduce the impact that fear can have on vulnerability. Aiming too high or having unrealistic expectations of ourselves can lead to being overwhelmed and frustrated and can even destroy our self-trust because we begin to doubt our capabilities. None of this is good for vulnerability, but it sure does feed fear. One barrier to cultivating more realistic expectations is that much of the messaging we have received from society, family, and friends about both body image and sex promotes perfection as an attainable standard. The more we can dismantle this and challenge it, the easier it will become to be more vulnerable. For example, if you are expecting an orgasm from every single sexual encounter you have, that is an unrealistic expectation. This can cause you to resent your partner(s) or your body, and over time, you might even fear sexual encounters because they do not live up to your expectations. But if you shift your focus to a pleasure versus performance mindset, as we learned about in Chapter Six, it becomes less scary to be vulnerable and participate in sexual encounters in a fully present way.

Taking Sexy Back

An important aspect of body image that we have not yet talked about is sexualization. Sexualization occurs when women and women's bodies are made to be seen as nothing more than sexual objects. Essentially, when a woman is sexualized, the worth of her body is directly equated to its potential sexual function. This happens both within the context of our interpersonal relationships and our media consumption. Interpersonally, this can be things like unwanted advances, comments about our bodies, catcalls, and stares. In the media, sexualization shows up in the form of sexually objectifying behaviors and images that are found everywhere, from our social media feeds to print ads, TV shows, movies, and song lyrics. The examples are endless, but one that comes to mind is the Carl's Jr. ad campaign circa 2010-2015 that featured both print and TV commercials of nearly naked women holding cheeseburgers with sexually suggestive poses and looks. Sexualization leads to many problems, including anxiety about appearance, increased feelings of shame, and body image issues[32].

In terms of vulnerability and redefining sexy, it is important to distinguish the difference between being sexualized and being sexy or sexual. Being sexualized or objectified is not something a woman chooses. Being sexy or sexual is completely your choice, is defined personally, and is something that can be an essential part of a healthy body image and satisfying sex life. When we get to choose how to express our own sexuality, our body image and sexual satisfaction levels both start to improve.

Being sexy or sexual means different things to different people. It's important to consider:

How would you define sexy?

When do you feel sexy?

How does the way you feel about your body impact your ability to feel sexy?

If you do not know the answers to these questions right now, that is okay. You can figure it out by being vulnerable, leaning in, and trying new things. Some ways to explore what sexy is to you are spending more time nude, wearing lingerie or different types of undergarments, using the dimensions of touch exercise from chapter one, and just generally doing things outside of your norm when it comes to your sexuality.

Another thing to consider is creating a sexy vision board. You may have heard of a traditional vision board, which is a collage of images that integrates photos, drawings, affirmations, and mantras that people create to help inspire and motivate them. The sexy vision board is similar, but the focus is not on life and career goals. Instead, it is on helping you to create and manifest your best sexual life. When looking for images for your sexy vision board, ask yourself:

What does your sexual life look like with a more positive body image?

Where are you?

Who are you with?

How does it feel?

What do you need for that to happen?

Another way to reclaim sexy for yourself and explore what that means to you is by using photography. You can have your partner(s) take sexy photos of you, you can take sexy selfies, or you can even go to a professional photo studio for a boudoir session. Boudoir sessions are a relatively new trend in photography in which you hire a professional photographer to take intimate photos of you wearing lingerie in sexy poses. These sessions have emerged as an excellent way to see your body from a different perspective and gain confidence, but admittedly, they can be pricey. In Appendix D, I have included a link to a site that has some fantastic tips for taking sexy selfies that can help you create your own boudoir session if it's out of reach financially or if you aren't quite ready to have your photos taken by a stranger. These tips can also be helpful if you choose to have your partner(s) take the photos.

Regardless of the method you choose for taking sexy photos, try to be mindful during your session and be intentional about connecting to your body and looking at it in a more kind and gentle way. Uncomfortable feelings may come up during these experiences, but focus on using some of the skills you have learned in the book to lean into vulnerability and fear and to process the feelings that come up rather than letting them stop you.

Summing It Up

Vulnerability is the final component of great sex that we are focusing on in this book.

Being vulnerable requires bringing together many of the skills and concepts you have learned throughout the book.

Being able to trust both yourself and your partner(s) is important for cultivating vulnerability.

Part of trusting yourself is knowing your strengths.

Part of trusting your partner(s) comes from sharing.

Fear can be a roadblock to vulnerability - if we let it.

Being afraid of something does not mean we shouldn't (or can't) do it.

Reclaiming your sexy is an important part of being vulnerable.

Conclusion

The End of the Road

Wow! We have been on quite the journey together as we have navigated our way to learning how a better body image can help with experiencing better sex. We have learned about so many things, from mindfulness to identifying values, to challenging your negative thoughts, to creating a sexual menu, and so much more. And now, here we are at the end of the road. Through this journey, you have had to do a lot of hard work, which may have felt deeply uncomfortable at times. And that is a good thing! In fact, I am really hoping that you *were* uncomfortable at times because discomfort is often how we find the motivation to grow and make lasting changes.

Despite this being the end of the book, it isn't likely the end of your journey to improve your body image or to experience better sex. This road may be ending, but it is not a dead end. As most journeys tend to be, it isn't necessarily going to go along a straight path – there will be twists and turns along the way. Some days are going to be harder than others because when we continue to experience the messaging from society, family, and friends that our bodies are not good enough, we will undoubtedly, at times, allow that messaging to impact how we talk to ourselves and treat ourselves, which means we are continuously reinjuring our body image. But when you can use the resources and exercises in this book to pause and start to be kinder to yourself and to understand yourself better, you will grow stronger over time, and those new injuries will heal much faster.

Remember, this is a process. We didn't wake up one day hating our bodies and letting that hate impact our sex lives negatively. It took time. It seeped in slowly the more we learned about the standards of beauty our patriarchal society was dumping on us. It crept in as we listened to our family and friends talk about their own bodies and judge the bodies of those around us. It worked its way into our minds every time we watched our mother or friend or another female role model go on yet another diet. We learned it as we watched the pretty skinny girls on TV and in movies easily get the most attractive partners and have hot, satisfying sex with them. So, just as that all took time, it will take time to undo. But you *can* undo it. You *can* unravel it bit by bit and piece by piece by using the tools in this book. You *can* practice mindfulness and cultivate empathy. You *can* name your shame instead of hiding from it. You *can* speak up for yourself and ask for what you need. You *can* challenge your thoughts and rise above them. You *can* explore your turn-ons and define what sexy is to you. These are some ways that you can continue to wipe away the messaging and create a new life in which your body image does not define you or your sex life.

Sharing is also part of the journey. Share this book with a friend or family member. Share your experiences- be vulnerable and let others know they are not alone. You just might be surprised at the things they share with you in return. As Brené says - the more we talk and the more we can be vulnerable, the more we can dismantle shame.

Despite my hope that your body image has started to improve and you are having better sex through the work you have done by reading this book, I realize this is still just a book. It is not therapy and cannot replace starting or continuing the work with a great therapist. If you don't already have one, please use the resources in Appendix B to help find one. Also, speaking of the appendices, they include a variety of websites, apps, and book recommendations. Rest assured that these recommendations are vetted – either I or my clients have used them and found them to be helpful. Please make use of this resource, as these tools can greatly supplement what you have already learned by reading this book.

I feel torn as I write these final words– as endings are bittersweet. I want to leave you with profound words of wisdom. I want to make you sweeping promises and provide assurances that we can conquer body image issues once and for all – all in the name of better sex. Unfortunately, I don't think I can do that because loving all of your body all of the time is probably not a realistic expectation in this society. Sadly, I just don't think it is possible. But what I can do is instill hope and reinforce to you that you are not alone. Change *is* possible. You *can* feel differently about your body and have better sex as a result.

I will leave you with this: a poem I came across during my research for this book. It is one I love and hope you will too:

> Today I asked my body what she needed,
> Which is a big deal
> Considering my journey of
> Not Really Asking That Much.
>
> I thought she might need more water.
> Or protein.
> Or greens.
> Or yoga.
> Or supplements.
> Or movement.
>
> But as I stood in the shower
> Reflecting on her stretch marks,
> Her roundness where I would like flatness,
> Her softness where I would like firmness,
> All those conditioned wishes
> That form a bundle of
> Never-Quite-Right-Ness,
> She whispered very gently:
>
> Could you just love me like this?
>
> -Hollie Holden[33]

Endnotes

Chapter One

Tseng, J., Poppenk, J. (2020). Brain meta-state transitions demarcate thoughts across task contexts exposing the mental noise of trait neuroticism. *Nature Communications.* 3480 ,11.

Kleinplatz, P. J., Menard, A. D., Paquet, M.-P., Paradis, N., Campbell, M., Zuccarino, D., & Mehak, L. (2009). The components of optimal sexuality: A portrait of "great sex." *The Canadian Journal of Human Sexuality,* 18(1-2), 1–13.

McCarthy, B. & McCarthy, E. (2019). *Enhancing Couple Sexuality: Creating an Intimate and Erotic Bond.* Routledge.

Chapter Two

El-Hamamsy, D., Parmar, C., Shoop-Worrall, S., & Reid, F. M. (2022). Public understanding of female genital anatomy and pelvic organ prolapse (POP); a questionnaire-based pilot study. *International urogynecology journal,* 33(2), 309–318

Hunt, A. & McGinley C. What does a normal vagina look like? A no-nonsense guide to vaginas and vulvas. *Woman and Home.* https://www.womanandhome.com/health-and-wellbeing/normal-vagina-what-is-a-vulva-

Hunt, A. & McGinley C. What does a normal vagina look like? A no-nonsense guide to vaginas and vulvas. *Woman and Home.* https://www.womanandhome.com/health-and-wellbeing/normal-vagina-what-is-a-vulva-

Teixeira, A. L. S., Damasceno, V. O., Dias, M. R. C., Lamounier, J. A., & Gardner, R. M. (2013). Association between Different Phases of Menstrual Cycle and Body Image Measures of Perceived Size, Ideal Size, and Body Dissatisfaction. *Perceptual and Motor Skills*, 117(3), 892–902.

Mostova, O., Stolarski, M., & Matthews (2022). I love the way you love me: Responding to a partner's love language preference boosts satisfaction in romantic heterosexual couples. *PLoS ONE* 17(6).

Chapter Three

Brown, B. (2012). *Daring Greatly: How the Courage to Be Vulnerable Transforms the Way We Live, Love, Parent, and Lead*. Avery: An Imprint of Penguin Random House.

Brown, B. (2006). Shame Resilience Theory: A Grounded Theory Study on Women and Shame. *Families in Society*, 87(1), 43–52.

Brown, B. (2012). *Daring Greatly: How the Courage to Be Vulnerable Transforms the Way We Live, Love, Parent, and Lead*. Avery: An Imprint of Penguin Random House.

Fletcher, J. (2023, April 17). *Why Do Humans Have Pubic Hair?* https://www.medicalnewstoday.com.

Chapter Four

Uvnäs-Moberg, K., Handlin, L., & Petersson, M. (2015). Self-soothing behaviors with particular reference to oxytocin release induced by non-noxious sensory stimulation. *Frontiers in Psychology*, 5, 1529.

Chapter Five

Levine, M.P. & Chapman, K. (2011). Media Influences on Body Image. In T. Cash & L. Smolak. (Eds.), *Body Image: A Handbook of Science, Practice, and Prevention* (pp. 101-109). Chapter, The Guilford Press.

Common Sense Media (2015). *Children, Teens, Media, and Body Image: A Common Sense Media Research Brief*. https://www.commonsensemedia.org

Stice, E., & Shaw, H. E. (1994). Adverse effects of the media portrayed thin-ideal on women and linkages to bulimic symptomatology. *Journal of Social and Clinical Psychology*, 13(3), 288–308.

Papp, I., Urban, R., Czegledi, E., Babusa, B., Tury, F. (2013). Testing the Tripartite Influence Model of body image and eating disturbance among Hungarian adolescents. *Body Image*, 10, 232-242.

Kamps, C.L. & Berman, S. L. (2011). Body image and identity formation: the role of identity distress. *Revista Latinoamericana de Psicología,* 43(2), 267-277.

Chapter Six

Messerly, J. G. (2017). Summary of Maslow on self-transcendence. *Institute for Ethics and Emerging Technologies.* https://www.reasonandmeaning.com.

Adapted from: Berman, R. (October 28, 2022). *The Missing Apex of Maslow's Hierarchy Could Save Us All.* https://www.freethink.com.

Reed, P. (1987). *Self-Transcendence Scale.*

Ackard, D.M., Kearney-Cooke, A., Peterson, C.B. (2020). Effect of body image and self-image on women's sexual behaviors [Research Summary]. *The Canada Journal of Human Sexuality,* 9 (2).

McCarthy, B. & Farr, E. (2012). Strategies and Techniques to Maintain Sexual Desire. *Journal of Contemporary Psychotherapy.* 42: 227-233.

Nagoski, E. (2015). *Come As You Are: The Surprising New Science That Will Transform Your Sex Life.* Simon & Schuster, Inc.

Chapter Seven

Janssen, E., & Bancroft, J. (2007). The dual control model: The role of sexual inhibition and excitation in sexual arousal and behavior. In E. Janssen (Ed.), *The psychophysiology of sex* (pp. 222–197). Indiana University Press.

Nagoski, E. (2015). *Come As You Are: The Surprising New Science That Will Transform Your Sex Life.* Simon & Schuster, Inc.

Lehmiller, J. (2020). *Tell Me What You Want: The Science of Sexual Desire and How it Can Help You Improve Your Sex Life.* hachette go.

Cook-Cottone, C.P. (2015). Incorporating positive body image into the treatment of eating disorders: A model for attunement and mindful self-care. *Body Image.*

Chapter Eight

https://www.merriam-webster.com/

Brown, B. (2012). *Daring Greatly: How the Courage to Be Vulnerable Transforms the Way We Live, Love, Parent, and Lead.* Avery: An Imprint of Penguin Random House.

Fishbane, M. (May 27, 2015). *Cultivating Connection: Reviving the Lost Art of Eye Contact.* http://www.goodtherapy.org

Solomon, A. H. (2020). *Taking Sexy Back: How to Own Your Sexuality & Create the Relationships You Want.* New Harbinger Publications.

Conclusion

Holden, Hollie. (2016, June 30). Today I asked my body what she needed, Which is a big deal Considering my journey of Not Really Asking [Image Attached] [Status Update]. Facebook. https://www.facebook.com/hollieholdenlove/photos/a.388682557915623/990659447717928/?paipv=0&eav=AfadSE7MK3lpboWUWwQ5428yFEdOLWtpc-dh1LYv-LARK_VyTjE6w9-fJ2gV24GN63vg&_rdr

Appendix A: Grounding Skills

Grounding and Emotional Regulation Skills - Use these when the work that you are doing starts to feel too intense or overwhelming.

Four Square Breathing. Begin by slowly exhaling all of your air out. Then, gently inhale through your nose to a slow count of 4. Hold at the top of the breath for a count of 4. Then gently exhale through your mouth for a count of 4. At the bottom of the breath, pause and hold for the count of 4.

Say a safety statement. "My name is ____. I am safe right now. I am in the present. Not the past. I am located in ____. The date is ____."

Describe your environment in detail using all your senses. Describe objects, sounds, textures, colors, smells, shapes, numbers, and temperature. You can do this anywhere. For example, on the subway: "I'm on the subway. Those are the windows. This is the bench. The metal bar is silver. The subway map has four colors..."

Imagine yourself leaving the painful feelings behind. Picture yourself: gathering the emotions, balling them up, and putting them into a box, walking, swimming, biking, or jogging away from painful feelings, or imagining your thoughts as a song or TV show you dislike, changing the channel or turning down the volume — they're still there, but you don't have to listen to them.

Run cool or warm water over your hands/splash your face

Grab tightly onto your chair as hard as you can.

Touch various objects around you: a pen, keys, your clothing, the table, the walls. Notice the textures, colors, materials, weight, and temperature. Compare the objects you touch.

Dig your heels into the floor. Literally grounding them. Notice the tension centered in your heels as you do this. Remind yourself that you are connected to the ground.

Jump up and down. This one might sound silly, but research shows that this lowers stress hormones and increases endorphins!

Say kind statements as if you were talking to a small child. E.g., "You're a good person going through a hard time. You'll get through this."

Think of favorites. Think of your favorite color, animal, season, food, time of day, or TV show.

Picture people you care about. E.g., Your children, friends, pets, and look at photographs of them, imagine their voice and them telling you that the moment is tough but that you'll get through it.

Practice gratitude, identify the things you are grateful for – overall or specific things that have happened today, write or think of five things that bring you joy

Appendix B: Mental Health Resources

Mental Health Resources

To find a therapist:

Inclusive Therapists offer a safer, simpler way to find a social justice-oriented counselor, therapist, or coach.

https://www.inclusivetherapists.com/

Psychology Today's Find a Therapist Feature:

https://www.psychologytoday.com/us

Good Therapy's Therapist Directory:

https://www.goodtherapy.org/find-therapist.html

American Association of Sexuality Educators, Counselors, and Therapists Referral Directory:

https://www.aasect.org/referral-directory

In a Crisis:

National Hopeline Network: 1-800-SUICIDE

The Trans Lifeline – Dedicated to the well-being of trans people: 877-565-8860

Crisis Text Line - Text GO to 741741

Appendix C: Book Recommendations by Chapter

Introduction

Magnificent Sex: Lessons from Extraordinary Lovers by Peggy J. Kleinplatz, PhD and A. Dana Menard, PhD - Written from the research on the principles of great sex that this book is organized on

Chapter One

Better Sex Through Mindfulness: How Women Can Cultivate Desire by Lori A Brotto, PhD – Provides more information on the research behind mindfulness as well as additional mindfulness exercises

Chapter Two

The 5 Love Languages: The Secret to Love that Lasts by Gary Chapman – Detailed descriptions of each of the love languages and the 5 Love Languages Profile to help you determine your love language

Chapter Three

Daring Greatly (or anything!) by Brené Brown – Deconstructs shame and urges readers to find ways to be vulnerable and challenge their fears

Our Bodies, Ourselves - An amazing compendium from The Boston Women's Health Book Collective that covers everything from anatomy to body image to sexuality to menopause to the politics of women's health

The Body is Not an Apology by Sonya Renee Taylor – Introduces the concept of body terrorism or the war on bodies and offers tools and guidance for radical self-love

Beautiful You: A daily guide to radical self-acceptance by Rosie Molinary – A beautiful book with daily prompts empowering women to redefine beauty and improve self-esteem

Chapter Four

Sensate Focus in Sex Therapy by Linda Weiner and Constance Avery-Clark – This is a more clinical book but provides an excellent step-by-step description of a full sensate exercise with beautiful illustrations

Burnout: The Secret to Unlocking the Stress Cycle by Emily Nagoski and Amelia Nagoski – Provides a great explanation of the inner critic or "madwoman in the attic" and why befriending her is a good idea

Chapter Five

The Body Positivity Card Deck: 53 Strategies for Body Acceptance, Appreciation, and Respect by Judith Matz and Amy Pershing – A 53-card deck with healing strategies designed around building self-confidence and respect for your body

The Body Image Workbook: An Eight-Step Program for Learning to Life Your Looks by Thomas Cash – CBT-based exercises to help you feel more confident in your body

Chapter Six

Come as You Are: The Surprising Science That Will Transform Your Sex Life by Emily Nagoski – A guide to understanding women's sexuality and creating a sex life filled with confidence and satisfaction

The Body Liberation Project: How Understanding Racism and Diet Culture Helps Cultivate Joy and Build Collective Freedom by Chrissy King – Provides information on body liberation as well as personal antidotes and exercises designed to help everyone find body liberation

Health at Every Size: The Surprising Truth About Your Weight by Lindo Bacon – Utilizes research and scientific data to inform about the health at any size movement while encouraging body acceptance

Finding Your Sexual Voice: Celebrating Female Sexuality by Barry McCarthy and Emily McCarthy - Each chapter includes a detailed psychosexual exercise, as well as a range of motivating case studies, to help women discover their sexual style and value their sexual voice

More Than A Body: Your Body is an Instrument, Not an Ornament by Lexie Kite and Lindsay Kite - Powerful and practical advice that goes beyond "body positivity" to help readers develop body image resilience

Chapter Seven

Tell Me What You Want: The Science of Sexual Desire and How it Can Help You Improve Your Sex Life by Justin Lehmiller – Provides data on people's sexual fantasies to help you better understand your own sexual desires

Reclaiming Pleasure: A Sex-Positive Guide for Moving Past Sexual Trauma and Living a Passionate Life by Holly Richmond, Ph.D. – Offers survivors of sexual assault practical tools to help cultivate the safety, security, and trust needed in order to experience sexual pleasure

Chapter Eight

The Power of Vulnerability by Brené Brown – Encourages readers to look at vulnerability as a strength, not a weakness

Appendix D: Additional Resources by Chapter

Chapter One

Women's Sensual Body Meditation Script – an audio and print script of a guided meditation focusing on finding sensuality in your body.

https://womensmeditationnetwork.com/your-sensual-body-sexuality-morning-meditation-mm/

Chapter Two

The Labia Library – everything you wanted to know about your labia, includes a link to the labia photo gallery, which is a wonderful way to see a wide range of diverse labia.

https://labialibrary.org.au/your-labia/

Chapter Three

Dr. Kristen Neff's website about self-compassion. LOADED with exercises and resources. I especially love the guided practice recordings.

https://self-compassion.org/

Chapter Four

OMG yes – Pay once for a lifetime subscription to this website, which gives access to hundreds of interview and demo videos dedicated to learning about pleasure, including how to ask for it.

https://start.omgyes.com/join

Dipsea – An app with short and sexy audio erotic stories written by women that are great for masturbating to. Find it in the app store on your phone.

Sex toys:

https://www.goodvibes.com

https://www.babeland.com

https://hoelisticshop.com

How to choose a lube:

https://drbrighten.com/what-to-avoid-in-a-lube

Chapter Five

Activism initiatives you can get involved with, plus lots of other body image resources:

https://bodyimagemovement.com

Chapter Six

Pamela Reed's Self-Transcendence Scale:

https://nursologycom.files.wordpress.com/2018/10/sts-2018.pdf

Chapter Seven

Emily Nagoski's Sexual Temperament Questionnaire:

https://static1.squarespace.com/static/5a2311d41f-318d2a02e64554/t/6041263453b09545f885239a/1614882356439/Sexual%2BTemperament%2BQuestionnaire.pdf

A variety of "Yes/No/Maybe" Checklists – These can help to explore sexual interests that you might have never considered. Use alone or with your partner(s).

https://willsexcoach.weebly.com/uploads/1/2/4/6/124623137/yes_no_maybe_checklist.pdf

https://www.scarleteen.com/sites/files/scarleteen/ynmPDF.pdf

https://www.autostraddle.com/wp-content/uploads/2014/06/sexa-palooza-handout-branded.pdf

Spicer – An app to use with partners to explore sexual interests and find matches in a fun and non-threatening way. Find it in the app store on your phone.

Ethical Porn Sites/Sources:

Make Love Not Porn: https://makelovenotporn.tv/

Lust Cinema: https://lustcinema.com/

Bright Desire: https://brightdesire.com/

Bellesa: https://www.bellesa.co/

List of physical activity ideas:

https://heatherfit.ca/2021/10/11/100-ways-to-be-physically-active-ultimate-list-of-physical-activities/

Chapter Eight

Evergreen – an app that can help with a couple's communication. Find it in the app store on your phone.

This website is overall cis-hetero-centric, but has some great ideas for making sexy selfie-taking more fun:

https://badgirlsbible.com/how-to-take-a-sexy-selfie

www.ingramcontent.com/pod-product-compliance
Lightning Source LLC
Chambersburg PA
CBHW071717020426

42333CB00017B/2301